# Harvey Steiman's California Kitchen

## The KCBS Kitchen Cookbook

Harvey Steiman

*Foreword by Jeff Smith, The Frugal Gourmet*

*Chronicle Books · San Francisco*

## DEDICATION

*For Al Hart, who makes me
sound good;*

*And my wife, Carol,
without whom my life would
be much less savory.*

Printed in the United States of America.

Library of Congress Cataloging-in-Publication
Data

Steiman, Harvey.
    [California kitchen]
    Harvey Steiman's California kitchen : the
KCBS Kitchen cookbook / Harvey Steiman.
        p.    cm.
    ISBN 0-87701-689-5
    1. Cookery, American—California style.
    2. KCBS Kitchen (Radio program)
    I. Title.    II. Title: California kitchen.
TX715.2.C34S74    1990
641.59794—dc20                    90-1829
                                  CIP

Editing: Pat Tompkins
Cover photograph: Will Mosgrove
Book design: Ingalls + Associates
Composition: Wilsted & Taylor

Distributed in Canada by
Raincoast Books
112 East Third Avenue
Vancouver, B.C. V5T 1C8

10  9  8  7  6  5  4  3  2  1

Chronicle Books
275 Fifth Street
San Francisco, California 94103

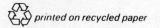 *printed on recycled paper*

# CONTENTS

# FOREWORD

By Jeff Smith
The Frugal Gourmet

I know a lot of wine snobs, people who feel that wine should be seen as a luxury rather than the necessity it is. And, I know a lot of food snobs, people who use the word "gourmet" as if it implies the ability to rise above the fact that food sustains us. If we don't eat, we die. Whether you live on caviar or chitterlings, the truth remains the same.

I have always liked Harvey Steiman. I knew him during the old days at the San Francisco *Examiner*, and we would go out to have lunch at some creative joint in the city, a joint that served fine food and always seemed to run short on pretension—perhaps a joint like Little Joe's on Broadway. Harvey and I would drink cheap wine and eat fish stew and boiled beef with green sauce. I loved it.

On a couple of occasions I was a guest in Big Harvey's home. He roasted small birds over fresh rosemary, but we still drank cheap wine.

You can imagine my discomfort when it was announced that Steiman was to take on the *Wine Spectator*, a journal read by those who really know their wine talk. I was afraid he had gone to the other side, that he had joined the wine snobs, that he believed that the Coming of the Messiah was going to take place in the Napa Valley. You can imagine how I felt. I was afraid that I had lost a compatriot, a fellow searcher for good basic foods and wines that stand up to the attack of any arrogant judge.

As of the writing of this foreword I am happy to report that Harvey really has not changed much, he has just become more educated as to the true meaning of food and wine and the table. What a relief!

This book, which centers around his terribly popular radio food-talk show (Who else would even try such a thing and get away with it?) offers recipes that are both basic and creative. Real Big Harvey style. He even says that he doesn't like to use the word "cuisine" on the air. "It sounds too fancy, too intimidating!" He is still Harvey.

If you further doubt the basic value of this volume may I point out that the recipes run the whole kitchen line from Turkey Gravy (page 149) to Banana Crème Brulée (page 235), White Bean and Lentil Puree (page 229) and his Mother's squash recipe (page 188). Such a nice boy! And you must try the Baked Polenta and Prawns (page 137). Wonderful!

Our association has always been a delight. But, I have to admit that I am a bit nervous about this book. This is the best thing that Steiman has done, and he has several other books in his past. But look, I write cookbooks too, and I have two sons in college. His daughter is nowhere near college age. I just hope that he puts the money the book earns into a fund for his daughter.

# INTRODUCTION

Every morning between 10 and 11 o'clock some 300,000 listeners across Northern California tune their radios to KCBS to hear me talk with people about food, wine, and cooking. They phone from their homes, often from their own kitchens, sometimes from their offices, occasionally from their cars. Every once in a while they are so eager to get on the air and talk about what interests them about things gastronomic that they call from a pay phone. In most cases they want a piece of advice: they are planning a dinner party and wonder what to serve with the leg of lamb purchased at the butcher's; they have been making Aunt Hattie's sponge cake for years, but suddenly it's coming out lopsided; they just bought this strange but fascinating vegetable called arugula and wonder how to prepare it; they found a bottle of 1956 California Rhine Riesling and wonder if it's worth anything; they're in the market for a new skillet and wonder what the best choice is; or perhaps they have just returned from a vacation in Italy and want to know how to make that spaghetti *alla carretiera* that was so scrumptious in Rome. All of these questions have come up at one time or another in the nearly eight years I have been hosting the "KCBS Kitchen" for an hour every weekday. They are typical.

Please notice that there is no "cuisine" in the title of this book. Even in these days of California Cuisine, East-West Cuisine, Nouvelle Cuisine, this cuisine and that, seldom does the word *cuisine* pop up in my on-the-air conversations. It sounds too fancy, too intimidating. Technically, *cuisine* is only the French word for *kitchen*, but in the English language it suggests something more serious, a codified way of cooking, an almost intellectualized approach to food. We tend to forget that all good food happens in a kitchen, and it is always done best by people who enjoy being there. During that one hour on the radio every morning, our world centers on what goes on in the kitchen. My listeners and I explore the practical aspects of preparing that food well: shopping, storing, cooking, and eating. We share ideas for finding better food, keeping it better, making it more imaginative, and finding a few shortcuts to make the going easier. Sometimes we have guests, including some of the best-known cooks and writers in the food world. The guest list has included Julia Child, James Beard, Wolfgang Puck, Jacques Pepin, Paul Prudhomme, Paula Wolfert, Marcella Hazan, Laurel Flinders, Bert Greene, Craig Claiborne, William Rice, and Marian Burros.

And every day, I offer a recipe. Usually it is something I have cooked recently. Sometimes it is a dish encountered at a restaurant, or a friend's home, that struck me as particularly charming or tasty. Sometimes it is an example from a new cookbook I review that day. When a guest joins us, he or she almost always shares a recipe. Most often it is something seasonal, either because it has a connection with an approaching holiday or because it takes advantage of the first fresh asparagus to hit the market or of the height of strawberry season. This book is a collection of those recipes.

All of these recipes have several things in common, dictated in part by the restrictions of sharing them over the radio. I discovered very early that recipes with long lists of ingredients only confused listeners trying to jot them down as I spoke. Therefore, the vast majority of the recipes in this book use six or fewer measured ingredients (salt and pepper don't count); virtually all the rest use fewer than ten. Also, the directions for putting the ingredients together should take no more than three or four minutes to explain. The ideal radio recipe contains three ingredients and takes several minutes to describe.

Surprisingly, these restrictions have not stifled creative possibilities in the least. Most recipes with long lists of ingredients are little more than variations on a basic theme; the author has simply added some seasonings, specified garnishes, or combined several smaller recipes to make one big one. I firmly believe that real creativity is more than playing with the seasonings; it's getting to the heart of a dish and expressing its essence in your own terms. That usually does not require a huge arsenal of ingredients. What it does require is imagination in combining flavors or refining techniques to make food taste the way you want it to.

The proof is in the mailbox. Listeners can send self-addressed stamped envelopes for any recipe I give on the "KCBS Kitchen." Two hundred to 250 requests for each recipe are not uncommon. In addition, each week the *San Francisco Chronicle* food section publishes all the recipes offered on the "KCBS Kitchen" from the previous week. If there is ever a typographical error in any of those recipes, published or mailed, we hear about it. People don't just listen passively to these recipes; they cook them. If something is wrong, which blessedly is seldom, I hear about it. As a result, each recipe has been thoroughly tested by thousands of listeners.

In more ways than they know, these listeners are the lifeblood of the program. Not only do their questions and comments set the tone and direction of the daily conversation but their choice of topics also suggests recipe ideas for future programs. Sometimes it is as obvious as a request for a particular dish. One day, a listener phoned to inquire in a wistful tone if I remembered Blum's Coffee Crunch Cake. Blum's was a San Francisco institution in another era, a fancy ice-cream fountain and tearoom, and that cake was a mainstay. Not having that recipe in my files, I said so on the air. By the end of the week, the mailbag was overflowing with recipes, some clipped from old newspapers, others typed on 3 × 5 cards, others painstakingly written out in longhand. I tried several of the more likely candidates, took the best of them, and read the result during a later broadcast. It is one of the most requested recipes we've ever offered. (See page 274 for the final version.) Sometimes, the influence on these recipes is less clear. By the questions asked, I can detect an interest in a new ingredient or cooking technique and provide a recipe that ties into that interest. In an important sense, these recipes therefore represent the way Northern Californians really cook at home. If there is a California Cuisine, maybe this is it.

As a journalist, I understand why the notion of a California Cuisine carries a certain allure. After all, it's something to write about. But the reality is that California will never have a cuisine in the same way that Provence, Tuscany, or Shanghai have cuisines. Those cuisines developed in relative isolation, before the jet plane made it possible to buy fresh ingredients from virtually every corner of the globe and electronic communications made it possible to read about the latest developments in French nouvelle cuisine before the chefs knew what it was. Today, California's cooks are too aware of too many influences to create such a unique statement. But we do have our own style in Northern California, and I believe this collection of recipes reflects that style.

We also like to drink wine with our meals in Northern California. According to some statistics I've seen, Bay Area residents drink about twice as much wine per capita than anywhere else in the United States. Proximity to some of the world's finest vineyards has something to do with that pleasant practice, but I also think it's part of the Northern California style to appreciate the taste of a good wine with good food. In this book, I have put on my wine writer's hat and suggested certain types of wines that in my experience enhance the enjoyment of these dishes. Do not feel constrained to follow these ideas slavishly. They are only suggestions. Besides, when my wife and I feel like drinking a Pinot Noir, we go ahead and drink it even though the classical accompaniment to the food on our plates should be Chardonnay. Feel free to do the same.

I mentioned that I am a journalist. When listeners to the radio program meet me for the first time, they often ask if I have been a chef. Sometimes they even tell me how much they enjoyed my restaurant. I have never been a chef, nor have I had a restaurant. My career in journalism started in the sports department of the *Los Angeles Times*, where I worked as a copy boy to earn enough money to go to college. I studied music, but the steady work seemed to be in journalism. That led me to a career writing about food and wine.

During my four years as a desk editor in the sports department of the *Miami Herald*, the newspaper's regular part-time restaurant critic retired. Having dabbled in the kitchen since I discovered good food was too expensive to eat in restaurants on a newspaperman's salary, I asked for some assignments. Later, when the *Herald* wanted a new food editor, I escaped the sports department for the kitchen. Using standard journalistic technique, I asked every expert I met every question I could think of. Blessed with a Velcro brain, I managed to learn quite a bit about food. In 1977 I became the *San Francisco Examiner's* food and wine editor.

Newspaper food editors have a special relationship with readers. Readers phone for advice. They ask questions about menus, fallen cakes, strange vegetables, and unfamiliar wines and dishes they have encountered in restaurants. It occurred to me as I chatted with them that other people might enjoy eavesdropping on these conversations. I brought the idea to KCBS. The station was already broadcasting a food program of sorts, a half hour a day with Joe Carcione, the greengrocer of TV and radio fame. Nobody knew the ins and outs of sweet corn better than Joe, but people wanted to ask questions about cooking, too. On March 1, 1982, the first "KCBS Kitchen" went on the air as a supplement to Joe's half hour. By June 1, the programs were combined into an hour-long daily broadcast. As the program became more popular and Joe's health became less robust, his portion dwindled to a half hour a week. He kept it up until a few weeks before his death from cancer in 1988.

There is a precedent for the "KCBS Kitchen." When I was growing up in Los Angeles in the 1960s, I used to listen to Mike Roy carry on similar conversations about cooking with his listeners on KNX. He had an avuncular manner with listeners, putting them at their ease as they shared ideas and questions with him. I learned as much about food listening to him as I did watching Julia Child's pioneering television program. Mike Roy was still doing the daily program when he died in 1977. I only hope that KCBS listeners are as eager to rush to the kitchen and cook something after listening to me as I was listening to him.

# What the Low-Fat Symbol Means

This is not a diet book, nor is it intended to be. Because most of us are either watching our waistlines or trying to eat healthier, however, we are conscious of how much fat we use. Recipes in this book that naturally use little or no fat or that suggest alternative methods for removing some of the fat are marked with this symbol.

Although these recipes are not designed for very low-calorie diets, they generally contain fewer calories than similar dishes. It is possible to reduce the oil or butter in many other recipes, although the character of the finished dish could be compromised. If you are on a special diet, try cutting back on the fat and see how you like it.

# QUESTIONS AND ANSWERS

One of the most appealing aspects of the "KCBS Kitchen" is that neither I nor the listeners quite know what's coming next. Someone might want help sorting out a cooking technique or a confusing element of a recipe. Often it's about an unfamiliar ingredient or how to make substitutions for health or economy. About one in fifteen questions is about wine.

Sometimes the questions come out of left field, such as the caller who wanted a more elegant way to chip pieces off a 10-pound chocolate bar besides using a hammer and chisel (I suggested sawing with a serrated knife) or another who wondered how a jet flight would affect his wine (I assured him that wines do not get jet lag). Two of my favorites are from the caller who wondered if he could use his microwave oven to kill the bugs he found in his bulk spices and another who wanted to make a Jell-O mold in the shape of a piano. I said no to the bugs. All you have to do is sift them out. For the piano mold, I suggested making up an extra-thick batch of mashed potatoes from dried potato flakes and forming the curvature of the piano in a flat pan, then lining the cavity with plastic wrap. A caterer phoned the next day to suggest that the caller cut Styrofoam to the desired shape and line with plastic wrap, because potatoes can become pockmarked.

Occasionally, there are callers who are a bit unclear on the concept. In all innocence they ask questions that would do Mrs. Malaprop proud. One of my favorites was the 12-year-old girl who couldn't figure out why her cake frosting recipes called for "tartar sauce." Could she use corn syrup instead? I asked her to read the recipe to me. The ingredient in question was cream of tartar, which I explained was a powder to be added to the egg whites to keep them firm. Another caller wondered if it would be right to make chocolate chip cookies for a reformed alcoholic. It seems all the chocolate chips listed "chocolate liquor" among the ingredients. I explained that chocolate liquor is nothing but the paste formed by grinding up the cocoa beans in the chocolate-making process and that it contained no alcohol.

Most queries are more practical. Throughout the book are fifty of the most often-asked questions, culled from actual calls in the past few years.

# CHAPTER ONE:

# BEGINNINGS

# BEGINNINGS

There was a time when having a bite to eat before a meal as a means of whetting the appetite struck me as self-defeating. If you're going to put some effort into the main course or courses, why ruin everyone's appetite by giving them something to chew on before they ever get to the table? Perhaps my ears were still ringing with my mother's admonition, "Don't eat so much bread or you won't finish your meal."

But a good appetizer doesn't ruin your appetite. It just takes the edge off raging hunger so that, when you do sit down to the main course, you don't feel like tearing into it. You can appreciate the food better if there is a gradual crescendo and decrescendo to a meal, something the French, Italians, and Chinese, to name the practitioners of three of the world's most advanced cuisines, have known for centuries. Like a warmup act at a concert or comedy performance, a small taste of something savory gets the menu rolling gently, building up nicely to the main attraction without overshadowing it.

The key, of course, is to keep it small, whether the dish in question is to be consumed as the first course at table or eaten along with a cocktail or glass of wine while guests are gathering. Huge servings of appetizers are a mistake. They should not satiate, but leave you wanting more. That is the psychological and physiological reason behind a first course. For this same reason, the best first courses avoid too much meat, poultry, fish, or cheese, all of which tend to satisfy one's appetite in relatively small quantities.

Soups make excellent starters for several reasons. For one thing, they can usually be prepared in advance and therefore present little or no problem for the host of a dinner party. Also, being liquid, a soup doesn't seem "filling." Brothy or lightly thickened soups are the best choices. Thickened potages or cream soups are OK if they are not too thick or creamy; if they are, they should be served in small quantities. Soups that are basically thin stews, such as bouillabaisse, are really one-dish meals; they should be served as main courses.

Wines for appetizers should be light and refreshing. Don't worry about matching wines to ingredients. What counts is the weight of the wine. Champagne is a popular choice at this point of the meal because it plays all the right notes—it's light, crisp, and delicate in texture, and the bubbles are appetizing. I also like fresh, young wines, including fruity reds such as Beaujolais or Dolcetto at this stage of a meal. This is the time for any white wine that is *not* aged in wood, including dry or slightly sweet Rieslings, Gewürztraminers, and Chenin Blancs. Save the heavier Chardonnays, white Burgundies, and oak-aged Sauvignon Blancs for later courses where they can perform their magic with a full plate of food.

# Prawns in Mustard Tomato Sauce

*I like to prepare this dish before the guests arrive and serve it at room temperature as a first course with a good bottle of Chardonnay, preferably one with one or two years of age on it. In Northern California, big shrimp are called prawns.*

1 pound extra-large (or jumbo)
  prawns
1 shallot, finely chopped
1 tablespoon olive oil
1 pound ripe tomatoes, fresh or
  canned, peeled, and finely chopped
¼ cup dry white wine
2 tablespoons Dijon mustard
Salt and freshly ground pepper

Peel and devein the prawns. Set them aside. In a large skillet, over low heat, cook the shallots in the olive oil for about 1 minute. Turn up the heat and add the tomatoes. Cook uncovered 2 to 3 minutes until the tomatoes start to dry. Add the wine and prawns; cook over moderate heat 3 to 5 minutes. Remove the prawns and arrange on plates or a platter. Stir in the mustard. Add salt and pepper to taste. Pour the sauce over the prawns. Makes 4 to 6 appetizer servings.

> **Q.** *You recently described a fast way to make tomato puree. Can you go through it again?*
>
> **A.** This is a method I learned from Paula Wolfert, a New York food writer, who learned it from a cook in Southwest France. Use the coarse side of a four-sided grater, or a flat grater placed on top of a bowl. Cut the tomatoes in half crosswise and squeeze out the seeds and jelly. Rub the flat side of the tomato against the grater. Don't worry. The skin of the tomato protects your fingers from being grated along with the tomato. And it grates so fast, you won't bother to use the food processor unless you need quarts of the stuff.

# Spinach Pinwheels

*These pinwheels of biscuit dough filled with spinach and blue cheese make delicious finger food. They are also good with a soup or salad for a light lunch, or use them as the base for creamed chicken or turkey. They taste fine at room temperature to take along on a picnic or pack in a box lunch.*

Preheat the oven to 425° F., and generously grease a large baking sheet.

Stir together the flour, baking powder, salt, pepper, and nutmeg. Blend in the butter until the mixture is crumbly—just like mixing a pie crust. Your fingertips are the best tools for the job, but you can also use a food processor. Add the milk, stirring with a fork just until the mixture comes together in a rough mass. Turn out onto a lightly floured surface, and knead gently about 8 times, then push, pat, and roll the dough into a rectangle 10 by 8 inches, keeping the corners as square as possible. Spread the surface with the spinach, then sprinkle on the cheese. Starting at one of the long ends, roll the dough up like a carpet. With a sharp knife, cut the tube of dough into pieces about ¾-inch wide.

Place the pinwheels, barely touching, on the prepared baking sheet and bake for about 15 minutes, until puffy and browned. Some of them may stick to the sheet a bit if the cheese has melted and bubbled onto the baking pan; just get under them with a spatula, and they'll come off. Makes about 15 pinwheels.

2 cups flour
4 teaspoons baking powder
½ teaspoon salt
¼ teaspoon freshly ground pepper
¼ teaspoon nutmeg
5⅓ tablespoons (⅔ stick) room temperature butter
⅔ cup milk
½ cup cooked, chopped spinach, well drained
½ cup (about 3 ounces) crumbled blue cheese

# Tomato Tart

*The season's first rain in California usually means the end of tomatoes for home gardeners, leaving the vines full of green or partially ripened fruit. The tomatoes for this tart should be ripe but firm—even slightly green. This tart, sweet, spicy and easy to assemble, has a flavor different from the familiar raw tomatoes in salads.*

Basic pastry for a 9-inch pie or tart
   shell (page 298)
¼ cup flour
⅓ cup packed brown sugar
½ teaspoon ground cinnamon
3 or 4 tomatoes (about 1 pound)
2 tablespoons butter

Preheat the oven to 425° F.

On a floured surface, roll out the pastry and fit it into a 9-inch pie or tart pan. Trim any overhanging edges.

Stir together the flour, sugar, and cinnamon; set aside. Cut the stem end from each tomato, then slice tomatoes about ⅛-inch thick. Arrange half the slices in an overlapping circular pattern in the bottom of the tart shell. Sprinkle with all but 2 tablespoons of the flour-sugar mixture. Arrange the remaining slices on top in a circular pattern and sprinkle with remaining flour-sugar mixture. Dot with the butter. Bake for 35 to 45 minutes, until the edges of the crust have browned and the tomato juices are bubbling and slightly thickened. Serve warm or at room temperature. Makes 6 servings.

# Real Onion Dip

*Most of us are so accustomed to onion dip being made from packaged onion soup mix and sour cream that it's easy to forget how the idea originated. Try the difference.*

Place the onions in a nonstick or heavy aluminum skillet, cover, and cook over low heat for about 20 minutes, stirring occasionally, until wilted. Uncover and continue cooking gently for about 45 more minutes, until very soft, sweet, and reduced to just a fraction of their original volume. Cool to room temperature, then stir in the remaining ingredients, adding salt and pepper to taste. This is good with potato chips and also as an omelet filling. Makes about 2 cups.

**2 pounds yellow onions, thinly sliced (about 6 medium)**
**¾ cup sour cream**
**4 ounces cream cheese at room temperature**
**1 teaspoon Worcestershire sauce**
**Several drops Tabasco**
**Salt and freshly ground pepper**

# Eggplant Appetizers

*This is an easy way to cook eggplant without using an inordinate amount of oil. To make finger food with this recipe, cut each "sandwich" in quarters, holding the pieces together with toothpicks before the final baking. A little fresh tomato sauce is good with these as an appetizer.*

1 large eggplant
About ¼ cup olive oil
6 thin slices Provolone or jack cheese
1 egg, beaten
About ⅔ cup bread crumbs
1 teaspoon dried oregano, thyme, or
   basil (or 1 tablespoon fresh)
1 teaspoon salt
¼ teaspoon freshly ground pepper

Cut the eggplant crosswise into ¼-inch slices. You should be able to get 12 slices out of the middle of a large eggplant. (Save the ends to add to pasta sauces or omelets.) If the eggplant is fresh, its flesh will have a greenish caste. If it is not that fresh, sprinkle the slices with salt and let them stand for 30 minutes to remove any bitterness. Rinse and pat dry.

Preheat the oven to 450° F.

Brush each slice with olive oil, and make sandwiches of 2 eggplant slices and a thin slice of cheese. Trim any excess cheese to fit. Dip the sandwiches in the beaten egg, then in the bread crumbs mixed with the remaining seasonings. Arrange the eggplant sandwiches on an oiled or nonstick baking sheet.

Bake the eggplant sandwiches for 10 to 15 minutes on each side. They should be well browned. They can be served hot, but I think they're best at room temperature. Serve 1 per person as an appetizer (6 servings), 3 as a main dish (2 servings).

# California Dungeness Crab Cakes

*I came up with this recipe to serve to friends visiting from Italy to give them a taste of something distinctly Californian. There is nothing quite like California Dungeness crab, but if you must substitute blue crab or some other species, make sure it is as fresh as possible.*

Cook the crab and let it cool. Shell and pick the crabmeat. Chop the onion and dice the bell pepper fine. Sauté them in the butter. When they are soft, combine them with the crabmeat, the bread crumbs and the eggs beaten with the mustard. Toss the mixture together with the parsley. Form it into 6 patties and arrange them on a piece of wax paper. Cover with plastic wrap and refrigerate for at least 1 hour.

Just before serving, panfry the patties in a mixture of 2 tablespoons butter and 2 tablespoons vegetable oil until they are brown on both sides, about 3 minutes per side. They will be very fragile. Don't worry if they fall apart; just form them back into patties on the plate. Serve with lemon wedges and a sauce made by blending a heaping tablespoon of mustard (such as the type used in this recipe) into a cup of sour cream, if you like. Makes 6 appetizer servings.

1 Dungeness crab, about 2 pounds
1 small onion, chopped
1 medium bell pepper, chopped (red preferred)
2 tablespoons butter
¾ cup bread crumbs
2 eggs
1 teaspoon Dijon mustard or California-style sweet hot mustard (such as Mendocino or Napa Valley brands)
¼ cup chopped parsley
Butter and oil for frying

# Rillettes of Chicken and Pork

*A sort of primitive pâté,* rillettes *are a homey, tasty spread to serve with cocktails or on a picnic, spread on French bread or crackers, with mustard and tart pickles on the side.*

1 ½ pounds boneless lean pork
1 pound boneless, skinless chicken
  breasts
2 cups chicken broth
1 ½ cups dry white wine
1 onion, halved
1 bay leaf
4 cloves garlic
½ cup olive oil
Salt and freshly ground pepper
Freshly ground nutmeg

Combine the pork, chicken, broth, wine, onion, bay leaf, and 2 of the cloves of garlic in a large saucepan. Bring to a boil, cover, reduce heat, and simmer for about 3 hours, until the meat is meltingly tender. Discard the onion and bay leaf; with a slotted spoon transfer the meat to a food processor fitted with the steel blade. Reserve cooking liquid.

Add the remaining 2 cloves of garlic to the meats, and process with several on-off pulses until the mixture is finely chopped. With the machine running, slowly pour in the olive oil. The mixture should be firm enough to hold its shape in a spoon but not stiff and dry. If it seems quite dry, whirl in several spoonfuls of the cooking liquid to moisten. Season to taste with salt, pepper, and nutmeg, and chill before serving. Makes about 4 cups.

# Chicken Liver Pâté

*The tartness and hint of sweetness provided by the apples give this spreadable pâté its special character. Use green Pippin or Granny Smith apples for best results.*

In a heavy skillet, melt 3 tablespoons of the butter over high heat. When the foam subsides, add the onion and apple. Sauté the mixture until the apple is soft enough to mash with a spoon. Pour the contents of the skillet into a blender or food processor.

Melt 4 tablespoons of the remaining butter in the skillet and brown the livers, about 5 minutes. They should be firm but still a little pink in the middle. Add the brandy and ignite it. Let the flames subside and pour the contents into the blender with the apples and onions.

Add the remaining 3 tablespoons butter and the cream to the mixture. Blend it until it is very smooth, scraping down the sides of the blender or food processor as necessary. Season the pâté to taste with the nutmeg, salt and pepper.

Pour the mixture into a 3- or 4-cup soufflé dish and or mound it onto a plate. Cover it tightly with plastic wrap, and chill it in the refrigerator. For longer storage, rub the warm surface with butter to form a coating of fat. It will store up to a week in the refrigerator. It also freezes well.

Garnish the pâté with parsley; serve with crackers or toast. Makes about 4 cups.

10 tablespoons (1 stick plus 2 tablespoons) butter
½ cup chopped onions or shallots
2 small, tart apples, peeled and diced
1 pound chicken livers
3 tablespoons brandy
1½ tablespoons lemon juice
2 tablespoons whipping cream
¼ teaspoon freshly grated nutmeg
Salt and freshly ground pepper
Parsley for garnish

# Cucumber-Mustard Ring

*This may seem like an old-fashioned church-supper appetizer, but the flavors are so fresh and appealing that even the trendiest modernist will succumb to its charms. Use less mustard for a milder salad; the full amount will make it spicy hot.*

2 large cucumbers (about 1 pound), peeled, halved lengthwise, and seeded

1 envelope unflavored gelatin

½ cup sugar

2 to 3 tablespoons dry mustard

½ teaspoon salt

⅔ cup white-wine vinegar or cider vinegar

4 eggs

1 cup whipping cream

Grate the cucumber halves, then squeeze out the shreds a handful at a time. Reserve the excess liquid from the shreds. Sprinkle the gelatin over the reserved cucumber juice. After about 5 minutes, when the gelatin has softened, dissolve it either by microwaving at 70 to 80 percent power for about 1 minute or stirring it in a small pan over low heat for 1 to 2 minutes.

In a medium saucepan combine the sugar, mustard, and salt. Whisk in the vinegar and eggs, then the dissolved gelatin. Cook over medium heat, stirring constantly, for about 5 minutes, until the mixture thickens slightly but does not come close to a boil. Chill until the mixture mounds slightly when dropped from a spoon.

Whip the cream and fold it in along with the cucumber shreds. Pour into a 6-cup ring mold (or other mold), and chill for several hours. Unmold onto a platter before serving. (To make the unmolding go smoothly, dip the bottom of the mold into a larger bowl of hot water for a few seconds. Dry it on a clean towel before inverting onto a plate.) Makes 6 servings.

# Date and Cheese Stuffed Phyllo Triangles

*The rich sweetness of the dates plays a balancing game with the savory flavor of the blue cheese, which has the desired effect of a good appetizer—to get the juices flowing.*

Beat together the cheese and pecans until completely blended. Fold in the chopped dates.

Preheat the oven to 350° F.

Brush 1 sheet of phyllo with melted butter, top with another sheet, and brush lightly again with butter. (Keep any phyllo you aren't working on covered with a damp towel.) Cut the buttered sheets into fifths across the shorter side. Place a teaspoon of the date mixture in the center of the first strip, just below the top. Fold a top corner across the filling to make a triangular shape, then continue folding down, over and over, just like folding a flag, as it forms a neat triangle.

Fill and fold the remaining strips the same way. Place on a baking sheet. Form the other triangles the same way with the remaining sheets of phyllo. Brush the tops with melted butter, and bake for about 15 to 20 minutes, until well browned. Serve hot or warm. Makes 40.

½ pound blue cheese, crumbled
½ cup chopped pecans
¼ pound moist pitted dates, chopped (about 1 cup)
16 sheets phyllo dough (about ½ pound)
8 tablespoons (1 stick) melted butter, plus a little more if needed

# Phil Q's Goat-cheese Spreads

*Phil Quatriciocchi owns a very successful cheese-distributing business. On a visit to the "KCBS Kitchen," he offered these quick spreads, which have become very popular around our house for informal gatherings. A Sauvignon Blanc is a fine companion.*

**5 ounces Sonoma goat cheese (one small round)**
**8 sun-dried tomatoes**

Allow cheese to come to room temperature. Blot all the oil from the sun-dried tomatoes. Puree in a blender or food processor. Slice a French bread baguette (not sourdough) ¼-inch thick, butter the slices lightly, and brown them in the oven until just crisp. Let them cool and serve them spread with the mixture.

*Variation:* In place of the tomatoes, use ½ ounce of black truffle peelings, well drained. Use cream cheese or any soft, fresh goat cheeses.

Q. *What is the best way to reconstitute dried tomatoes?*

A. Put them in a jar with a few sprinkles of water. Use 1 tablespoon for each cup of dry tomatoes. When all the water is absorbed, soak them in olive oil for a few hours. Instead of using water, you can flavor the tomatoes with vinegar, garlic and herbs.

# Salted, Sugared Nuts

*This was one of those cases when a listener wanted to know how to prepare this, I didn't know, said so, and then was inundated with letters and clippings explaining the technique. This is a distillation of several methods.*

Whisk the egg white and water together in a small bowl until blended. In a pie pan or on a plate, combine the sugar, salt, and cinnamon. A small handful at a time, dip the nuts in the egg white. Remove them with a slotted spoon, letting the excess drip back into the bowl. Roll and toss in the sugar mixture until coated.

*Conventional method:* Line a baking sheet with foil. Arrange the prepared nuts on it. Set in an oven preheated to 225° F. and bake for about 1 hour 15 minutes; the sugar coating should dry, but not brown much at all, so keep an eye on them, especially the last 15 minutes. Transfer the nuts to a rack to cool, then store airtight.

*Microwave method:* Arrange the prepared nuts in a single layer on a microwave-safe dish. Microwave on high for 3 minutes; the coating will froth and bubble up and look almost alive! Remove the nuts, and when the frothing subsides, transfer to a rack to cool, then store airtight. Makes about 2 cups.

1 egg white
1 tablespoon water
1 cup sugar
1½ teaspoons salt
1½ teaspoons cinnamon
½ pound pecan halves (about 2 cups)

# Acorn Squash and Apple Soup

*This soup captures the taste of autumn with minimal fuss. It is especially delicious served cold with a dollop of sour cream. To make a lower-calorie version, use half the butter and garnish with yogurt.*

½ medium onion, chopped
1 small acorn squash, peeled and
  seeded
4 tablespoons (½ stick) butter
1½ cups apple juice
1½ cups chicken stock
1 small apple, peeled and cored
Salt, white pepper, and sugar to taste
Sour cream for garnish (optional)
Chopped parsley for garnish

Sauté the onion and squash in the butter for 2 minutes. Add the apple juice, chicken stock, apple and seasoning. Cook until vegetables are tender, then puree in blender. Serve warm with sour cream on side. Garnish with parsley. Can be served hot or cold. Makes 6 servings.

# Asparagus Soup

*When asparagus makes its first appearance of the season, I steam some of it for all in the family to eat with the fingers while standing in the kitchen. The next batch goes into this soup, a sure-fire winner even in the fanciest meals.*

Cut the asparagus tips so they are 2 to 2½ inches long. Boil them 5 minutes in the water. Remove the asparagus to cool but reserve the water. Meanwhile, cut the remaining asparagus stalks into 2-inch pieces.

In a large saucepan, melt the butter and sauté the onion until it is soft, a few minutes. Sprinkle the flour on the butter-onion mixture, stir it to blend, then add the reserved asparagus water, chicken broth and asparagus stalks. Gently boil the stalks until they are very tender, about 20 to 30 minutes. Puree the soup in a blender, food processor, or a food mill. Return the soup to a clean pan, add the half-and-half and asparagus tips to heat through, and season with salt and pepper. Do not let it boil. Serve it fresh. Makes 6 servings.

2 pounds asparagus
3 cups water
4 tablespoons (½ stick) butter
1 medium onion, chopped
1 tablespoon flour
3 cups chicken broth
⅔ cup half-and-half
Salt and freshly ground pepper

# Avgolemono Soup

*This Greek classic is so easy to make that you can throw it together at the last minute for a quick dinner starter or a late night snack.*

4 cups chicken broth
⅓ cup uncooked white rice
Juice of 1 lemon
2 tablespoons cornstarch
2 tablespoons sherry
2 eggs
Salt and freshly ground pepper

In a medium-size saucepan, combine the chicken broth and the rice. Bring to a boil, cover the pan, lower the heat, and let it simmer for 15 minutes to cook the rice.

In a small bowl, mix the lemon juice, sherry, and cornstarch until smooth. Stir this mixture into the simmering soup. Keep stirring until the soup thickens slightly. Season to taste with salt and pepper. Beat the eggs in the same small bowl. Stir the eggs into the soup. Do not let the mixture boil after the eggs have been added. Makes 4 to 6 first-course servings.

# Broccoli-Celery Root Soup

*Two of my favorite vegetables make a wonderful soup—and a low-calorie one at that. The creamy base of the soup comes from the puree of celery root and chicken broth, which envelops the fresh broccoli—added at the end to keep its texture firm. Don't be intimidated by celery root, surely one of the ugliest vegetables but well worth the effort to cut away the gnarly surface. Use the standard technique for peeling round things: cut off the top and bottom, stand it up like a barrel and pare off the exterior by cutting down on it.*

Combine the diced celery root and chicken stock in a large saucepan, cover, and boil for about 15 to 20 minutes, until the celery root is very tender. Puree half the mixture in a blender or food processor, then return it to the pan. Season with salt and pepper. Add the chopped broccoli, cover, and simmer about 10 to 15 minutes more, until the broccoli is tender. Correct seasoning. Just before serving , stir in the cream, if desired, and the parsley. Makes 6 servings.

2 large celery roots, peeled and diced
4 cups chicken stock
Salt and freshly ground pepper
2 cups finely chopped broccoli
    flowerets
¼ cup cream (optional)
2 tablespoons chopped parsley

# Celery Root-Onion Soup

*The earthy taste of celery root and onions transforms itself into something sweet and wonderful in this easily prepared soup.*

5 large onions (about 2 pounds), thinly sliced

2 tablespoons olive oil

Salt and freshly ground pepper

1 large celery root (about 1½ pounds), peeled and diced

5 cups beef broth

¼ cup cream (optional)

Combine the onions and olive oil in a large skillet over medium heat, cover, and cook for about 20 minutes, stirring occasionally, until wilted. Uncover, season with salt and pepper, and continue to cook slowly for about 40 minutes more, stirring now and then, until the onions are soft, sweet, and pale golden.

Meanwhile, in a large saucepan, simmer the celery root in the beef broth until tender, then puree in a blender or food processor until smooth. Stir in the onions, the cream, if desired, for a little enrichment, and season to taste with salt and pepper. Makes 8 servings.

# Cucumber and Tomato Soup with Avocado

*Many cold soups are rich with cream—but not this one. It's a refreshing combination of tomato and cucumber, thinned with yogurt and enriched with diced avocado. Once the ingredients are on hand, you can make this soup in less than 5 minutes.*

Peel the cucumbers, cut them in half lengthwise, seed them, and cut them into small chunks. Combine them in a blender or food processor with the tomato juice. Whirl until completely smooth. (Do this in two batches if necessary.) Pour into a bowl and whisk in the yogurt, Worcestershire, and Tabasco, then season with salt and pepper to taste. Chill thoroughly. Before serving, peel and pit the avocado, cut it into ¼-inch dice, and stir it into the soup. Serve in chilled bowls. Makes 6 to 8 servings.

2 large cucumbers
4 cups tomato juice
1 cup plain yogurt
1 tablespoon Worcestershire sauce
Dash Tabasco
Salt and freshly ground pepper
1 large, ripe avocado

# A Different Chicken Noodle Soup

*This makes a delicious light supper. It's fast, too, just the thing to put together when you're running late. Try a flavored soy sauce, such as mushroom or ginger soy. Fresh noodles are essential for this dish. For a different effect, try the Hot and Spicy Noodles (page 127).*

1 whole cooked chicken breast,
   skinned and boned
1 teaspoon Oriental sesame oil
2 tablespoons soy sauce
2 tablespoons sake (Japanese rice
   wine)
4 cups chicken broth
Salt and freshly ground pepper
1 package (14 to 16 ounces) fresh
   Japanese noodles or fresh
   fettuccine

First fill a large saucepan with water and bring it to a boil.
Cut the chicken into small strips. Combine with the sesame oil, soy sauce, and sake. Heat gently in a microwave oven for 90 seconds on full power or, covered, in a 350° F. oven for 10 minutes.

Meanwhile, bring the broth to a boil in a small saucepan. Season it to taste with salt and pepper. Keep it hot.

Boil the noodles in the large saucepan for 1 to 2 minutes, or until they are cooked through. Drain well and divide them among 4 large soup bowls. Divide the flavored chicken and any remaining sauce among the 4 soup bowls. Ladle in the boiling-hot broth. Makes 4 servings.

# Fresh Corn Soup

*The first fresh ears of corn that arrive in our house each season are steamed and eaten with a slather of butter. The next bagful might be turned into this summery soup. Those who have never cut the kernels from a corn cob may find the prospect daunting, but it isn't difficult at all. Messy, maybe, but not difficult.*

Shuck the corn, removing the silk. Cut off the stalks and set the cobs aside while you heat the milk in a large saucepan along with the onion and the pepper. (I like to add a pinch of celery seed at this time.)

Now, with a sharp knife, cut the kernels from the corn cobs. Do this over a plate to catch the corn "milk."

When the milk is steaming, remove the onion pieces and discard them. Transfer the corn kernels and their juices to the steaming milk. Simmer the soup for 10 minutes. Stir some of the hot liquid into the flour, blend it with a fork or a wire whisk until it is smooth, and stir the mixture into the soup to thicken it. Let the soup simmer for 5 minutes longer.

Season it to taste with salt. If the corn is not very sweet, add a teaspoon of sugar. Finish it with the cream or half-and-half. Serve it immediately. Makes 6 to 8 servings.

**6 ears very fresh corn**
**4 cups milk**
**½ onion, cut in 2 pieces**
**A few grinds of white or black pepper**
**5 tablespoons flour**
**Salt**
**Sugar, if necessary**
**1 cup whipping cream or half-and-half**

# Whole Garlic Summer Soup

*Garlic lovers know that thorough cooking of whole cloves results in sweet, buttery-soft garlic that mashes easily into a puree. By blending the soft garlic into the mixture, its gentle perfume permeates this soup.*

2 heads garlic
2 tablespoons olive oil
1 medium onion, sliced
4 cups chicken broth
¼ cup uncooked white rice
4 tomatoes
1 dozen fresh basil leaves
Salt and freshly ground pepper

Break up the heads of garlic. Discard the outer paper, but do not peel the cloves.

In a wide saucepan, heat the olive oil and sauté the onion slowly until it is soft. Add the whole garlic cloves, cover the pan, and let the garlic stew for 30 minutes or longer. It will brown slightly. Stir occasionally to prevent it from burning. The cooked cloves should pop easily when squeezed and form a soft paste. Let the garlic stand until it is cool enough to handle.

Meanwhile, boil the chicken broth and rice until the rice is soft, about 25 minutes. Peel, seed, and chop the tomatoes.

Pop the garlic from its peel into the onion, discard the peel, and combine the onion-garlic mixture with the chicken broth and rice in a blender or food processor. Puree the mixture and return it to the pan. If it is too thick, add more stock. Add the tomatoes and the whole basil leaves. Taste for salt and pepper. This soup can take a lot of pepper. Cook the soup for 5 to 10 minutes, and serve it with crisp-crusted bread or croutons. Makes 6 servings.

# Mystery Avocado Soup

*What's the mystery? Try asking your guests to identify the ingredients when you serve this soup. You will be amused at the guesses. Chances are no one will think of grapefruit juice, but it adds just the right touch of haunting sweetness and crisp acidity.*

Peel, halve and pit the avocados. Place them in a blender or food processor with the broth and grapefruit juice. Puree the mixture and add salt and pepper to taste. Adjust the broth and grapefruit juice to taste. Serve cold. Makes 4 to 6 servings.

3 medium avocados
2 cups chicken broth
1 cup freshly squeezed grapefruit juice
Salt and freshly ground pepper to taste

# Guacamole Soup

*The flavors of guacamole taste great when made into a soup. A few tortilla chips on the side add an amusing touch.*

Peel, halve, and pit the avocados. Put 3 of the avocado halves in a blender or food processor along with the stock, lime juice, and yogurt. Blend until smooth. Add the tomato and cilantro sprigs. Blend or process in several on-off flicks, just until the tomato is coarsely chopped but not pureed. Pour the soup into a bowl and season as highly as you wish with Tabasco and salt. Chop the remaining avocado half and stir it into the soup. Chill thoroughly before serving. Makes 4 to 6 servings.

2 large ripe avocados
3 cups chicken stock
1 tablespoon lime juice
⅔ cup plain yogurt
1 large tomato, peeled, halved, and seeded
¼ cup cilantro sprigs
Several drops Tabasco
Salt

# Fresh Tomato Soup

*My technique for making tomato puree is simplicity itself and it saves having to peel the tomatoes. Don't let the soup cook too long or the fresh flavors of the tomato and basil will be lost.*

2 pounds fresh ripe tomatoes
4 shallots
2 cloves garlic
4 tablespoons (½ stick) butter
¼ teaspoon baking soda
4 cups (1 quart) milk
Handful of fresh basil leaves
1 teaspoon salt
Pinch white pepper and sugar
¼ cup cooked rice

Cut the tomatoes in half without peeling them. Squeeze the seeds and jelly into the sink. Holding the tomatoes on the skin side, grate them on the coarse side of a grater. (The skin will not grate, and the tomato pulp will accumulate inside the grater.)

Chop the shallots and garlic very fine. Heat the butter in a large saucepan. Sauté the shallots and garlic until they are soft, about 2 minutes. Add the tomatoes and soda. When the mixture is hot, stir in the milk and basil. Add the salt, white pepper, and sugar.

Put the rice in a blender or food processor. Add ¼ cup of the soup and blend to a thin paste. Whisk this into the soup to thicken it. Delicious with a small spoonful of pesto floating on it. Makes 6 to 8 servings.

# Tuscan Tomato Soup

*Every Tuscan family has its own recipe for this soup. This is more or less what I had at a small trattoria in Florence. Tuscan bread, a sourdough bread made without salt, is available only in some specialty bakeries. Use ordinary sourdough in its place.*

Chop the garlic. Peel, seed, and chop the tomatoes. In a deep saucepan, sauté the garlic and tomatoes in the olive oil for 5 minutes. Add the basil and broth and heat to the boiling point. Remove it from the heat and add the bread pieces. Let the soup stand to absorb the bread, about 30 minutes.

Just before serving, give the soup a few healthy stirs with a large spoon and serve. It should be tepid, not hot or cold. Serve extra virgin olive oil on the side for drizzling on the soup. Makes 6 servings.

2 cloves garlic
2 pounds fresh red ripe tomatoes
½ cup olive oil
2 tablespoons freshly chopped basil
   or parsley
6 cups chicken broth
2 cups stale Tuscan bread or sourdough, torn into pieces

Q. *What is extra-virgin olive oil? Is it so much better than other kinds of olive oil to justify the high price?*

A. Terms such as *extra-virgin*, *virgin* and *pure* may seem preposterous but they really do have legal definitions based on the amount of oleic acid in the oil. The less acid, the better the oil. Extra-virgin has the least. Virgin oil is next best. Oils that have more acidity need to be chemically treated to lower their acidity; the result is called pure oil. A lot of the flavor is lost in the process, so, to make it taste better, manufacturers often add a small percentage of extra virgin oil to pure oil. Some pure oils are excellent values for cooking purposes. Use extra-virgin oil for things like salads, where the flavor will be most evident.

Another factor is the type of pressing. The best flavor comes from cold-pressed oil.

# Spinach-Ricotta Soup

*The trick here is not to cook the spinach, just heat it very quickly and make the puree as fine as possible. A food processor works, but this is one of the few cases where a blender is a better choice if you have one.*

**2 large or 3 smaller bunches of spinach**
**2 cups chicken broth**
**1 or 2 cloves garlic**
**1 cup ricotta**
**½ cup cream or milk**
**Salt and freshly ground pepper**

Wash the spinach well and remove the large, tough stems. Don't be too fussy about removing every last bit of the stems; the soup will be pureed. Shred or chop the spinach coarsely. You should have 4 cups, lightly packed.

Combine the spinach with the chicken broth, garlic, and ricotta in the blender. Blend on high speed for about 1 minute, scraping down the inside of the container with a spatula if necessary so all the ingredients are thoroughly blended.

Pour the soup into a saucepan. Add the cream or milk and the salt and pepper. Heat it just to a simmer. (If it boils, you lose that brilliant green color.) Serve warm or chilled. Makes 4 to 6 servings.

# Zucchini and Basil Soup

*Even though this soup is meatless, the shredded zucchini gives it a hearty and satisfying consistency. It is lightly thickened with potato and flavored just before serving with a pungent basil aioli. You can prepare both the soup and the aioli ahead, then combine them at the last minute.*

Cover the potatoes with the chicken stock in a medium saucepan, bring to a boil, cover, and simmer gently until potatoes are tender. Puree until smooth in a blender or food processor. Return to the saucepan, add the zucchini, and simmer for about 5 minutes. Season with salt and pepper. (If you prepare the vegetables ahead of time, reheat them before continuing below.)

Whirl the egg yolks, garlic, and fresh or dried basil together in a blender or food processor for about 1 minute. Slowly add the olive oil in a thin stream— you will have a mayonnaiselike sauce. Just before serving, whisk the aioli into the hot soup. Heat just to a simmer—do not boil. Any leftover soup is delicious cold, thinned with a little milk or stock. Makes 6 servings.

3 medium boiling potatoes (about
   1¼ pounds), peeled and sliced
3 cups chicken stock
Salt and freshly ground pepper
3 medium zucchini, coarsely grated
2 egg yolks
1 large clove garlic
½ cup fresh basil leaves or 2 teaspoons dried basil
¼ cup olive oil

---

Q. *What is the best way to keep olive oil from going rancid?*

A. The temptation is to keep the oil in the refrigerator, but olive oil producers tell me the condensation of moisture inside the bottle actually makes the oil spoil faster. To keep oil fresh, open only enough at one time to use within a month or two. One way to save money is to buy larger containers, which cost less per ounce. Once opened, oil in larger containers can spoil, so save some half-bottles, or buy them at a wine-making store. Decant the oil into these smaller bottles. Filled bottles of oil will keep for a year or more.

**Q.** *What knives do I need for a well-equipped kitchen?*

**A.** Don't stint on quality. Buy the best you can. You really only need three: a paring knife, a utility knife 6 or 7 inches long, and a chef's knife 9 or 10 inches long. High-carbon stainless steel is the best material; it holds an edge well and does not rust. Shop for knives that feel balanced and comfortable. You will also need a "steel" for honing the knives' edge between the times when you have them professionally sharpened, every six to eighteen months, depending on how often you use them.

The next knife to get is a serrated knife. Nothing cuts a tomato or a loaf of crusty bread better. After that, think about a boning knife if you like working with meat and poultry; a long, flexible fish filleting knife if you catch or buy whole fish; and a carving knife if you serve a lot of roasts. A pair of utility scissors or poultry shears are also helpful for many uses.

**Q.** *My wife and I can't quite finish a bottle of wine at dinner. What is the best way to save it for another time?*

**A.** There are plenty of products on the market that promise to keep your wine fresh after you recork it. The vacuum-pump type, I find, works only for a day or two. You can buy spray cans of pure nitrogen under the brand name Private Preserve that blanket the wine left in the bottle with the inert gas so it does not oxidize and spoil. I have kept wine for two or three weeks using this system.

But I like low-tech solutions best. Just freeze the wine. Put the cork into the bottle and *stand it up* in the freezer. (Don't lay it down because what had been the outer end of the cork can contaminate the wine and make it spoil.) When the wine is frozen, you can lay the wine on its side for more efficient storage. Thaw it at room temperature until the ice melts, or use the microwave oven (!). I find 3:45 on high will just about thaw a ¾ full bottle of frozen wine. Decant the wine, because the freezing process tends to produce a lot of harmless sediment and tartrate crystals. I have successfully frozen wine for as long as a year.

# CHAPTER TWO:

# MAIN COURSES

# MAIN COURSES

In compiling the recipes for this chapter, I was struck by how dramatically poultry and fish dishes outnumbered meat. I think this is an accurate reflection of two phenomena. First, for health reasons, most of us are eating more fish and poultry and less meat these days. Also, the less assertive natural flavors of fish, seafood, and chicken make a cook more creative—well, this cook, anyway.

Within the meat category, my recipe files hold more interesting pork and lamb dishes than those for beef. The reason, I think, is that I tend to like beef more or less unadorned. A good steak, a simple roast, or a meat loaf is more satisfying to me than many more elaborate beef dishes, whereas pork and lamb seem to need more attention in the form of seasonings and sauces.

I am also a firm believer in the simple approach to fish and seafood. Because they cook so quickly, the delicate flavor and texture of fish fillets and steaks need only salt and pepper and a judicious touch of complementary flavor, which is another reason why fish and seafood dishes show up so often on the "KCBS Kitchen." They are good radio recipes, with few ingredients and only a few simple steps to remember.

Poultry is another matter. I probably prepare a simple roast chicken more often for family dinners than anything else, but I also recognize that the adaptability of chicken to almost any flavor imaginable also makes it a perfect main ingredient for a cook with imagination. For this reason, you will find a wide range of chicken dishes in this chapter.

The main dish is the point in the meal to pull the cork on the most interesting wines you want to serve. We spend more time lingering over this course than any other until dessert and coffee, so the wine to drink with it should be worth paying some attention to. The main thing to remember in selecting a wine for main courses is to focus on seasonings and sauces. This is more important than whether the main ingredient is beef, lamb or chicken. Also, because main courses tend to have more flavor and more complex flavors than earlier courses, any wine you choose should be fuller bodied and more flavorful than anything that comes before it in the same meal. Finally, remember Steiman's First Rule of Food and Wine Matching: The odds are with you as long as the food is good and the wine is good, and the worst thing that can happen is that you will have to drink some water or nibble on bread between bites and sips.

Q. *What is the difference between London broil and chateaubriand?*

A. Well, if you see a cut of meat labeled as either one, ask the butcher what it really is, because there is no such cut. London broil is usually cut from the top round, but it could be flank steak or what is sometimes referred to as Jewish fillet. The recipe calls for broiling it rare and cutting it diagonally across the grain. True chateaubriand is cut from the center of the tenderloin (which, cut into steaks, is called filet mignon), pan-browned and roasted. What is often sold as "chateaubriand" in many California markets is cut from the top sirloin, not a bad piece of meat but not as tender and buttery as a true tenderloin.

# Aromatic Steamed Crab

*My usual method for cooking Dungeness crab is to throw the live crabs into a big pot of boiling salted water and serve them with a little bowl of melted butter or olive-oil mayonnaise. When you get tired of that, try steaming them over this aromatic mixture, which makes them a perfect foil for a fresh, dry Riesling. Allow 1 to 1½ pounds of crab in the shell per serving for a main course.*

**Steaming mixture:**
2 to 3 cups water
2 cloves garlic, crushed
2 green onions, crushed lightly
½ teaspoon coriander seed
½ teaspoon celery seed
½ teaspoon sesame seed
8 to 10 peppercorns
2 bay leaves, crumbled
2 cloves

Rinse the crabs and set them aside. Combine the remaining ingredients in the bottom of a steamer or in a large pot fitted with a steaming tray. Bring it to a boil and add the crabs. Let them steam 8 minutes for small ½-pound crabs, 15 to 20 minutes for larger Dungeness crabs. Serve them warm with or without melted butter for dipping.

# Mussels in Pilaf

*Unexpected flavors of ginger and cilantro give this pilaf an international character.*

Clean the mussels, scrubbing off the barnacles, and discard any that are open or that won't close when you nudge them. Chop the ginger and onion.

In a large saucepan, combine the mussels with the ginger, 2 tablespoons of the chopped onion, the cilantro, and white wine. (Optional: Add a healthy pinch of flaked red pepper.) Cover the pan and bring the liquid to a boil. When the mussels open wide, about 5 minutes, remove them from the pan to a bowl. Discard any that fail to open. Make sure all the juices remain in the pan.

Strain the juices into a measuring cup. There should be 2 cups. If there is less, add wine. If there is more, boil the juices to reduce the volume.

Wipe the pan clean and melt the butter in it. Sauté the remaining onion and the garlic. When the onion softens, add the rice and stir it around to coat it completely with the butter. Add the reserved mussel juices, including any in the mussel bowl. Bring the mixture to a boil, lower the heat, and cover the pot. Let it simmer 18 minutes.

Meanwhile, remove the mussels from the shells. Reserve some shells for garnish. When the rice is cooked, stir the mussels into it. Serve it lightly sprinkled with chopped parsley or cilantro and garnished with the shells. Serves 6 as an appetizer, 2 or 3 as an entrée.

**Mussels:**

1 quart mussels, in the shell (about 2 pounds)
1 tablespoon chopped fresh ginger
1 medium onion, chopped
6 to 8 stems cilantro
1 cup dry white wine

**Pilaf:**

2 tablespoons butter
1 clove garlic, chopped
1 cup uncooked white rice

# Baked Salmon with Poor Man's Sorrel Sauce

*Sorrel is a vegetable, although you would never know it from supermarket produce departments, which insist on selling it as an herb. It tends to be high priced and you cannot always find it. I developed this spinach-based alternative to achieve the same contrast of tartness against the richness of the salmon.*

½ cup (1 stick) butter

2 teaspoons vegetable oil

4 even-size salmon fillets, 7 to 8 ounces each

½ cup dry white wine

2 tablespoons minced shallots

2 to 3 tablespoons fresh lemon juice (1 lemon)

¼ cup fresh spinach (packed)

Preheat the oven to 450° F.

Cut butter into ¼-inch thick pats and refrigerate until cold. Brush the bottom of a baking pan with oil. Arrange salmon pieces in a single layer without touching each other. Bake just until fish is opaque throughout and feels firm to the touch when lightly pressed with the fingertip, 6 to 8 minutes.

While salmon is baking, work quickly to prepare sauce. Heat wine to boiling in medium-size, heavy saucepan. Boil until reduced to ¼ cup. Add shallots and lemon juice, then heat to boiling and stir in spinach.

Add the butter all at once. Cook over high heat, stirring constantly with a wooden spatula or spoon. When it just begins to boil, immediately remove from heat. Some of the butter will still be solid. Stir rapidly as you remove pan from heat. This procedure emulsifies the butter into a light-textured sauce.

Transfer salmon to heated serving platter. Pour sauce over salmon and serve immediately. Makes 4 servings.

# Salmon with Onion Cream

*Use sweet onions. The cumin gives a hint of duskiness to the sauce, which is lovely with salmon.*

Sprinkle the salmon fillets lightly with salt, pepper, and cumin. Spread them with olive oil and let stand at room temperature to marinate for an hour.

Peel the onions, trim off the stems and tips, and cut the onions in half lengthwise. Cut each half across the grain into sections, then cut with the grain into thin slices so the pieces are no more than an inch long.

In a large saucepan, over low heat, cook the onions in the olive oil until they are soft. Cook them over low heat, covered, stirring them every now and then. Add the cumin and the white wine. Boil the mixture until the liquid reduces to ¼ cup. Add the cream and let it simmer until the sauce is thick enough to coat the spoon. Season to taste with salt and pepper. Set the sauce aside while you bake the salmon.

Preheat the oven to 450° F.

Bake the salmon for 10 minutes per inch of thickness. (If the salmon is ¾-inch thick, bake for 7 minutes 30 seconds, for example.) Transfer the salmon to a high-sided platter, and pour the hot onion cream over it. Makes 4 servings.

**Salmon:**
1½ pounds salmon fillets
Salt, freshly ground pepper, ground cumin
Olive oil

**Sauce:**
1½ pounds sweet onions
2 tablespoons olive oil
½ teaspoon cumin powder
½ cup white wine
1 cup cream
Salt and white pepper

# Fennel Salmon

*A classic flavor matchup is the taste of fennel with fish, which gets an added boost in this dish with the addition of an anise liqueur (such as anisette or Sambuca).*

3 tablespoons fennel seed
½ teaspoon freshly ground pepper
½ teaspoon salt
½ cup olive oil
2 tablespoons anise liqueur or brandy
4 salmon steaks (8 ounces each)

Toast the fennel seeds in an iron skillet or heavy pan over medium-high heat for about 3 minutes, stirring and tossing them almost constantly. Do not let them burn. Crush the warm seeds with a mortar and pestle or in a saucer with the back of a spoon. Combine them in a small bowl with the pepper, salt, oil, and liqueur or brandy.

Coat the salmon steaks with this mixture. Cover and chill for several hours in the refrigerator. Pat the fish dry before grilling or broiling for 8 to 10 minutes, basting with the marinade once or twice. Makes 4 servings.

# Halibut with Parsley Sauce

*A variation on a dish served at Orso, a trattoria in New York's theater district, this is a quick method of preparing halibut fillets and their sauce all in the same pan. An Italian Pinot Grigio or dry Chenin Blanc make fine accompaniments that will stand up to the food's flavors.*

Remove the fillets from the refrigerator about 30 minutes before cooking them, if possible. Salt and pepper them lightly.

Finely chop the parsley and garlic; combine with the olive oil and anchovy paste. Stir in a tablespoon or so of the wine. Set the mixture aside.

In a skillet without exposed aluminum, preferably a nonstick pan, bring the cup of wine to a boil. Add the fillets, lower the heat, cover the pan, and let the fish simmer for 3 minutes. Turn the fish, add the reserved parsley mixture, and let the fish finish cooking, about 3 or 4 minutes longer. Remove the fish from the skillet.

Boil the sauce until the liquid is almost evaporated. It will form a creamy emulsion sauce. Spoon this green sauce over the fish. Serve with roasted potatoes or buttered pasta. Makes 4 servings.

**4 halibut fillets**
**Salt and freshly ground pepper**
**1 cup dry white wine**
**1 cup parsley leaves, packed**
**2 cloves garlic**
**2 tablespoons olive oil**
**2 teaspoons anchovy paste or 2
   mashed anchovies**
**Juice of ½ lemon**

# Italian Fish

*I had fish prepared like this at the restaurant Tortuga in Rovato, near Brescia, in northern Italy. Rovato is a cattle-processing town, but the seafood at this restaurant was exquisite. The chef, Domenico Gabucci, made this dish with* branzino, *a sort of Mediterranean sea bass. It is equally delicious with any delicate white fish fillets. Try this simple preparation.*

1 whole fish (3 to 4 pounds), such as sea bass or a large sole
1 cup white wine
2 ripe tomatoes
12 fresh basil leaves
Salt and white pepper
7 to 10 tablespoons extra-virgin olive oil

Steam the fish over the white wine until it just flakes, 10 to 15 minutes.

Meanwhile, peel, seed, and chop the tomatoes. Select the eight best looking basil leaves for garnish and chop the rest. Combine with the tomatoes and a drizzle of the olive oil, just enough to coat everything very lightly.

Have 4 dinner plates ready and warm.

When the fish is done, peel off the skin. With a spoon and fork, scrape the fish from the bone in large flakes. Arrange the flaked fish in a single layer in the middle of each plate. Season it lightly with salt and white pepper. Top each serving with one-fourth of the tomato mixture. Spoon olive oil around the fish and garnish with whole basil leaves.

Serve with a young, crisp Chardonnay. Makes 4 servings.

# Fish with Tomato Horseradish Sauce

*The horseradish provides more of a perfume than a flavor in this colorful dish. It is equally good hot, warm, or cold, which makes it perfect for picnics or summer meals.*

Heat the oil in a large skillet until quite hot—almost smoking. Cut the fish fillets into 4 pieces and season them to taste with salt and pepper. Cook for about 2 minutes on each side, just until cooked through. Remove to a warm platter while you complete the sauce.

Pour the fat from the pan, then return the pan to moderately high heat and pour in the wine. Let it boil for a moment while you scrape any browned bits off the bottom. Add the tomato and horseradish, stir to blend, then boil rapidly for 1 to 2 minutes, until the sauce thickens. Swirl in the dill or basil and spoon over the fish. Serve immediately, let it cool and serve at room temperature, or serve cold. Makes 4 servings.

2 tablespoons olive oil
1½ pounds snapper, cod, or other firm-textured fish fillets, about 1 inch thick
Salt and freshly ground pepper
½ cup dry white wine
1 cup peeled, seeded, chopped tomato
2 teaspoons prepared horseradish
1 tablespoon chopped fresh dill or basil

---

Q. *How can I get the "fishy" taste out of fish?*

A. My mother used to soak fish in milk for 30 to 45 minutes. It works beautifully.

---

**Q.** *Would it be too much overkill to have microwave, convection, and conventional ovens in my new kitchen?*

**A.** If you have the space, why not? They are not interchangeable. Convection ovens are regular ovens with fans that blow the air around inside them so that food cooks more evenly and develops a nice crust. Microwave ovens work by bombarding the food with microwave energy. The food then cooks in its own heat. Each type of oven performs better than the others for certain things. Convection ovens are great for baking bread and roasting meat or poultry, neither of which does particularly well in the microwave. Microwave ovens cook fish and vegetables beautifully, and they are convenient for many incidental jobs like melting butter or chocolate, softening ice cream or cooking rice.

Rather than having separate convection and conventional ovens, the best idea is to have a pair of convection ovens with switches to turn their fans on and off. That way they can double as conventional ovens.

# O. J. Fish

*The O. J. refers, of course, to the orange juice that is the basis of the sauce, which makes itself as the fish cooks, either in the oven or in the microwave.*

LOW CALORIE · LOW FAT ·

Place the fillets in a buttered baking dish (not a metal pan). Season with salt and pepper. Squeeze the juice of the orange over the fish, then dot the fish with butter. Let it marinate for 30 minutes.

Preheat the oven to 375° F. Bake the fish for 8 to 10 minutes, or microwave 6 to 7 minutes on 100 percent power or until the fish is barely done to your taste.

Pour off and save the sauce and finish it with a touch of lemon. Serve the fish with rice or pasta and a green vegetable. The sauce is to be poured over the fish, but it is also terrific on the rice. Makes 4 servings.

1½ pounds fish fillets (sea bass or snapper)
Salt and freshly ground pepper
1 orange
4 tablespoons (½ stick) butter
Lemon juice

---

# Easy Fish

*Mix a quick marinade, let it get acquainted with any type of fish fillets, then bake the fish for 10 minutes. Open a good bottle of white wine, and you can't go wrong.*

Blend together all ingredients except the fish fillets. Spread 1 tablespoon of the mixture on each fillet. Let them stand for 30 minutes at room temperature. Preheat the oven to 450° F. Bake for 8 to 10 minutes. Serve warm, with fresh broccoli and perhaps a spoonful of mashed potatoes. Makes 4 servings.

1 clove garlic
1 tablespoon finely chopped onion
½ teaspoon thyme leaves
Pinch oregano
2 tablespoons oil
1 tablespoon wine vinegar
4 fish fillets (5 or 6 ounces each)

# Steamed Fish with Its Own Juices

*This technique was the invention of a brilliant Italian chef whom I knew in Miami, Raymond Laudisio. He devised the method of crisscrossing the celery and carrots when he couldn't find an extra steamer basket. The vegetables also flavor the steaming juices, which become the basis for the sauce. Ingenious!*

4 ribs celery
2 long carrots
1 shallot
1 bay leaf
1 sprig fresh rosemary, fennel or
   tarragon or 1 teaspoon dried
1 cup dry white wine (approximately)
2 fish fillets or steaks
Salt and white pepper
½ cup whipping cream (optional)
2 tablespoons butter (optional)

Cut each rib of the celery lengthwise into 3 or 4 long sticks. Do the same with the carrots. Chop the shallot and put it in a deep skillet large enough to hold the fish fillets. Add the bay leaf and herbs. Make a bed of the carrots, all facing one direction like slats, separated by at least ¼ to ½ inch. (You may have to shorten some of them to fit.) Crisscross the carrots with the celery, also ¼ to ½ inch apart. This makes a raised platform of sorts for the fish.

Add the wine to the pan and bring it to a boil. Lay the fish on top of the celery, and sprinkle it with salt and white pepper. Cover the pan. Steam the fish over low to moderate heat. Timing depends on the thickness of the fillets. Figure 10 minutes for each inch of thickness.

When the fish is done, remove it from the pan to a warm plate. Strain the juices into a saucepan. For a low-calorie sauce, thicken them with 1 to 2 teaspoons arrowroot or cornstarch dissolved in a like amount of water. For a rich but light sauce, boil the juices until they reduce to 2 tablespoons, then add the cream and boil it until it is about as thick as very light custard sauce. Swirl in the butter and correct the seasonings, if necessary. Spoon this over the fish and serve it with a light Sauvignon Blanc or white Bordeaux wine.

# Mushroom-stuffed Fish Fillets

*Here is one easy way to make plain sole or flounder a little fancier.*
*Instead of rolling up the fish, with this recipe you just make a sandwich*
*of the stuffing between two fillets.*

Preheat the oven to 400° F.

Make the stuffing first. Chop the mushrooms, the fennel (or sweet anise), and garlic in a food processor. In a skillet, sauté the mixture in the butter. After the moisture evaporates, add the green onions. Cook 1 minute, then blend in the egg. Cook 30 seconds and remove from heat.

Lightly salt and pepper the fish fillets. Place half the fillets skin side up. Spoon a tablespoon or so of the mushroom stuffing on the skin-side-up fillets. Place a second fillet, skin side to the stuffing, on top of each one. (The skin must face the filling; otherwise the fillet may curl when cooked.)

Arrange the fillets in a baking pan large enough to hold them. Pour on the wine. Dot each fillet with a teaspoon of butter. Bake for 10 minutes.

Dissolve the cornstarch in the milk. When the fish is done, pour the juices in the pan into a small saucepan and thicken with the cornstarch liquid. Taste for seasoning.

Serve 2 "sandwiches" per person with the sauce spooned over the top. Rice makes a good accompaniment. Makes 4 main-course servings, 8 for first courses.

*Note:* This can be done with larger fillets, 8 to the pound. Use more stuffing for each pair of fillets, and increase the cooking time to 15 minutes.

**Stuffing:**
**8 large mushrooms**
**1 bulb fennel (or sweet anise)**
**2 cloves garlic**
**2 tablespoons butter**
**4 green onions, chopped**
**1 egg**

**Fish:**
**16 small, thin sole fillets (such as rex**
**sole), slightly more than 1 pound**
**Salt and freshly ground pepper**
**¾ cup dry white wine**
**8 teaspoons butter**
**1 teaspoon cornstarch**
**2 tablespoons milk**

# Meat Loaf with a Tang

*One of my most-requested recipes is this meat loaf. The veal and/or pork provides a smoother texture than the beef alone does, but the secret to a good texture is not to handle the final mixture too much.*

1 pound lean ground beef
1 pound ground veal or pork or half veal and half pork
1 small onion
1 clove garlic
1 teaspoon salt
1 heaping teaspoon Dijon mustard
½ teaspoon freshly ground black pepper
1 tablespoon ketchup or cocktail sauce
Pinch nutmeg
Dash Tabasco
Generous dash Worcestershire sauce
2 eggs
⅔ cup bread crumbs soaked in milk

Place the ground meats in a large bowl. Very finely chop the onion and garlic—a food processor does this effectively—and add them to the meats along with the salt, Dijon mustard, pepper, ketchup, nutmeg, Tabasco and Worcestershire sauce.

Beat the eggs lightly—just enough to blend the yolk and white—and add them to the bowl. Drain the bread crumbs, squeeze them lightly, and add them to the mixture.

I prefer to use my hands to blend the mixture well. Hands are about the most effective tool, but if you're squeamish about it, use a spatula or a large spoon. Fold it together lightly, like a soufflé batter. Transfer it to an 8×4-inch loaf pan, or mold it into a rounded loaf shape on a baking pan. Bake the meat loaf at 350° F. for 1 hour 15 minutes.

Drain off the fat immediately. Serve it warm with mashed potatoes and gravy or a good tomato sauce. Have it cold on sandwiches the next day.

# Harvey's Chili

*The secret to good chili, to my way of thinking, is the aromatic ingredients, especially the cumin. The rest is balancing the hotness so that it does not completely overwhelm the senses. This dish always gets raves.*

Trim the visible fat from the beef. Dice the fat and put it in a skillet or deep casserole to melt. Or use ¼ cup vegetable oil. Meanwhile, dice, chop, or coarsely grind the meat.

When the fat has melted, discard the browned bits and any solids. Measure ¼ cup of fat and save the rest for another purpose. Lightly brown the onions, garlic, and green pepper in the fat. If using a skillet, transfer the mixture to a 5-quart pot.

Brown the beef in its own fat or in 3 to 4 tablespoons of vegetable oil. Drain the fat and add it to the pot. (If you do not render the fat as above, brown the onions, garlic, and pepper along with the beef.)

Add the remaining ingredients to the pot. If using canned tomatoes, chop the tomatoes roughly before adding them, along with the puree they are packed in. Stir the mixture well. Let it simmer, covered, for 3 hours, stirring the mixture occasionally. Taste for seasoning.

*Note:* You might want to wait until halfway through the cooking to add the *pequin* or cayenne pepper, and then do so a little at a time. The stuff is potent.

3 to 3½ pounds beef chuck or rump roast

2 teaspoons salt

½ teaspoon freshly ground black pepper

2 onions, diced

3 cloves garlic, finely chopped

1 green pepper, diced

1 can (15 or 16 ounces) tomato puree or tomatoes packed in puree

1 small can (4 ounces) diced mild green chilies

3 tablespoons mild red chili powder or sweet paprika (Hungarian or Spanish)

1 tablespoon hot red chili powder

1 small can ground cumin (about 1 ounce or 4 tablespoons)

1 teaspoon dried leaf oregano

1 teaspoon dried leaf thyme

½ teaspoon (adjust to taste) *pequin quebrado* or cayenne pepper

½ cup dry red wine

# Hamburgers with Olive and Sun-dried Tomato Sauce

*A colorful sauce of red wine, chopped olives, and that trendy ingredient of the 1980s, sun-dried tomatoes, dresses up the humble hamburger beautifully. Drink a hearty Zinfandel with your burger.*

1 pound ground beef
Salt and freshly ground pepper
2 tablespoons oil or shortening
½ cup red wine
½ cup beef stock or water
2 tablespoons minced sun-dried
   tomatoes (packed in oil)
2 tablespoons chopped black olives
   (either ordinary olives or the more
   pungent Mediterranean or Niçoise
   olives)
¼ cup whipping cream
2 tablespoons butter

Season the beef with salt and pepper and shape into four patties 3 to 4 inches in diameter. Heat the oil or shortening in a skillet over medium-high heat until almost smoking. Add the burgers and cook about 2 minutes a side for rare, 3 minutes a side for medium, or 4 minutes a side if you like them cooked all the way through. Transfer to a platter and keep warm for a few minutes.

Pour the browning fat from the pan and raise the heat to high. Pour in the wine and stock or water and boil rapidly, scraping the bottom of the pan, until the liquid is reduced by about half. Add the tomatoes and olives and boil a minute longer. Swirl in the butter and cream and boil until slightly thickened, then spoon over the burgers. Makes 4 servings.

# Mustard-glazed Corned Beef

*Tender, savory corned beef is delicious without any additions, but for a special presentation, try this mustardy glaze. It bakes on after the corned beef is thoroughly cooked, rather like glazing a ham.*

Rinse the corned beef, if it is still coated with salt. Place the pickling spice in a large saucepan or dutch oven. Put the corned beef on top of the spices, and add just enough water to cover the meat. Cover the pan, bring it to a boil, reduce the heat and simmer the corned beef for 3 to 4 hours, or until a fork slides easily in and out of it.

As an alternative, the corned beef may be steamed in a 300°F. oven for 3 to 4 hours in a covered roasting pan with 1 inch of water.

Trim off as much of the exterior fat as possible and place the corned beef on a roasting rack in a roasting pan. Make the glaze by blending the ingredients well. Spread the glaze over the exterior of the corned beef, and bake it at 350° F. for 20 minutes or so, or until the glaze is browned.

1 piece corned beef, brisket preferred, about 4 pounds
Water
1 to 2 teaspoons pickling spice (optional)

Glaze:
1 tablespoon butter, melted
2 tablespoons brown mustard
1 tablespoon brown sugar
Generous pinch ground allspice or small pinch ground cloves

**Q.** *How long should I cook a whole New York strip roast?*

**A.** Whatever you do, don't trust those roast-timing charts. At best they are only an approximation. They don't take into account the temperature of the meat when you start, which could vary by as much as 40 degrees, or the temperature of the oven, which could be off by as much as 50. But most important, what determines how long a piece of meat needs to cook is how thick it is, not how much it weighs. Weight works for birds, because they all have similar shapes, but a 10-pound roast is not going to take longer to cook than a 5-pound roast. Why? Because it is the same thickness, only longer.

Trust a meat thermometer inserted at the thickest point.

**Q.** *What is the best temperature for maximum tenderness of a roast?*

**A.** If it is a tender cut of meat suitable for roasting—essentially from the short loin or rib for beef or lamb—I recommend browning the meat at 450° F. for 25 minutes, then turning the heat down to 325° F. to finish cooking. Most cuts of meat are done to the rare stage in 1½ to 2½ hours.

Pork does not need the original browning. Just start it at 325° F. Pork can be taken out of the oven when the internal temperature reaches 155° F.

# Glazed Lamb Chops

*The Sonoma County Grape Growers Association offered this recipe, presumably to get people to use their Zinfandel. One tablespoon won't make much of a dent, so I suppose they want us to drink the rest of the bottle with this dish. It goes well.*

Trim excess fat from each chop. Score the fat edge with a knife to prevent curling while broiling. Place the chops on a broiler pan.

Sprinkle each chop with pepper. In a bowl combine the honey, mustard, and wine for a glaze. Brush the top side of each chop with the glaze mixture. Broil for 4 minutes. Turn the chops over, brush the second side with glaze, and broil for 3 to 4 minutes more. Do not overcook. Makes 6 servings.

**6 loin lamb chops, ¾- to 1-inch thick**
**Freshly ground black pepper**
**2 tablespoons honey**
**2 tablespoons Dijon mustard**
**1 tablespoon red or white Zinfandel**

Q. *What kind of wine should I put in a fancy lamb stew I am cooking for dinner?*

A. The rule of thumb on choosing a wine to use in a recipe is to select something you would be willing to drink yourself. Then go ahead and drink the rest of it with the food, if you like. This does not have to be a fancy, expensive wine, but don't use a bad wine for cooking. It just won't taste good.

# Pork Chops with Cider Sauce

*Browned quickly and then simmered briefly in cream and cider, even thick pork chops remain tender and juicy. Serve this with mashed potatoes and light white wine, like Muscadet or Chenin Blanc.*

4 pork chops, about 1½ inches thick
2 tablespoons vegetable oil (more, if needed)
Salt and freshly ground pepper
1 onion, very thinly sliced
½ cup cream or milk
½ cup apple cider or juice
2 tablespoons chopped parsley

Trim the pork chops of most of the visible fat. Heat the oil in a skillet over medium heat until it begins to smoke. Brown the chops 5 minutes on each side, sprinkling them with salt and pepper. Remove them to a platter.

There should be about 1 tablespoon fat left in the pan. If not, add a bit more oil and use it to cook the onion until it is wilted, about 5 minutes. Pour in the cream or milk and cider. Scrape the bottom of the pan to dissolve any browned bits.

Return the chops to the pan, along with any juice on the platter. Spoon the sauce over them and boil them gently, uncovered, to concentrate the sauce, for about 10 minutes, or until the chops are just barely cooked through. Taste the sauce, which should be slightly thickened, for salt and pepper.

Remove the chops to a platter or serving plates, spoon the sauce over them, and sprinkle them with parsley. Makes 4 servings.

# "Yorkshire" Pork Chops

*Because the Yorkshire pudding batter bakes in the same pan as the pork chops, it balloons up around the chops, becoming brown and crisp on the top and the bottom yet remaining soft, moist, and puddinglike inside. Don't use thin chops; they will become tough and dry in baking.*

Preheat the oven to 425° F.

Peel and core the apple, then slice it into 4 thick rings. Heat 3 tablespoons of the shortening or oil in a skillet with an ovenproof handle over moderately high heat. Quickly brown the apple rings for about 1 minute on each side. Remove the apples, and in the same fat (add a tablespoon more, if necessary) brown the chops for about 1 minute on each side. Place an apple ring on top of each chop and remove from heat.

Whisk together the milk, eggs, flour, butter, and salt until perfectly smooth. Pour the batter into the pan with the chops, and bake for about 25 minutes, or until golden brown and puffy. Take to the table and serve immediately from the pan, with apple sauce. Makes 4 servings.

1 large Golden Delicious apple
3 to 4 tablespoons vegetable shortening or oil
4 pork loin chops, about 1½ inches thick
1 cup milk
3 eggs
1 cup flour
2 tablespoons melted butter
½ teaspoon salt
Warm apple sauce

# Chicken Steeping Technique

*This is a great, simple way to prepare chicken for any dish that calls for cooked chicken, such as chicken salad, enchiladas, or soup. Because the chicken is cooking in ever-cooling water, it cannot overcook. It is one of my most-often-requested recipes.*

1. Use bone-in chicken breasts or thighs. Place them in a heavy saucepan so that they fill no more than half of the volume of the saucepan.
2. Pour cold water over the chicken to cover by 1½ inches.
3. Place the saucepan over high heat. Bring it to a boil.
4. Immediately turn off the heat, cover the pan tightly, and let the chicken steep for 20 minutes. Test the chicken for doneness by cutting along the keel bone with a sharp knife at the thickest part of the chicken. If it is no longer pink, the chicken is done.
5. If the chicken is still a little pink, bring it to a simmer. That should do it.

---

**Q.** *Would it be safe to clean chicken, cut it up and freeze it in a marinade for an upcoming camping trip?*

**A.** Yes, so long as the chicken does not thaw out too long before you cook it. If you have a refrigerator or ice chest to keep the chicken at a safe temperature, try freezing the chicken in plastic bags. They fit in the cooler better.

# Oven-baked Chicken Parmesan

*These oven-baked chicken pieces coated with a crispy, brown Parmesan cheese crust are especially delicious with baked or stewed tomatoes. Be sure to use freshly grated Parmesan—the packaged type becomes hard and pebbly looking when baked, rather than blending meltingly with the chicken.*

Preheat the oven to 350° F.

Stir and toss together the cheese, flour, oregano, and pepper, then dump out onto a pie plate or shallow platter.

Beat the eggs and water together. One at a time, dip each chicken piece into the egg mixture, shake off the excess, then roll in the cheese mixture. Arrange in a single layer in a baking dish. A 9 × 13-inch pan will hold the chicken comfortably. Dot each piece of chicken with about 1 teaspoon of butter. Bake for 1 hour, until chicken is cooked through. This is also good an hour later, after the chicken has cooled to room temperature, but has not yet been chilled. Makes 4 servings.

1 cup finely grated Parmesan
½ cup flour
1 teaspoon dried oregano or Italian seasoning
½ teaspoon freshly ground pepper
2 eggs
2 tablespoons water
1 chicken (about 4 pounds), cut up, or 4 pounds of assorted pieces
3 tablespoons butter

# Sherry Ginger Chicken

*Two of the key flavors in many Chinese stir-fries are just as delicious in a Western type of sauté.*

2 tablespoons olive oil or vegetable
  oil
4 skinless, boneless chicken breast
  halves (but not pounded)
Flour
Salt and freshly ground pepper
½ cup dry sherry
1 tablespoon grated fresh ginger (or
  less for a less pungent sauce)
2 tablespoons butter
1 tablespoon lemon juice
2 tablespoons chopped parsley

Heat the oil in a skillet over moderate heat until quite hot but not smoking. Dredge the chicken breasts in flour, and brown them for about 1 minute on each side in the hot oil, seasoning them lightly with salt and pepper. Reduce the heat to low and add the sherry and ginger to the pan. Swirl the pan to blend the ingredients, then cover and cook gently for 5 to 7 minutes, just until the chicken is cooked through. Uncover, and swirl in the butter, then the lemon juice.

Place the chicken on a warm platter, spoon on just enough sauce to moisten each serving, sprinkle with parsley, and serve. This is delicious with rice or potatoes. Makes 4 servings.

# Jack-Zucchini Chicken

*This layered dish of browned chicken breasts and zucchini topped with Jack cheese is great for company and takes only minutes to assemble. Serve with boiled potatoes, orzo (or other small pasta), or warm tortillas.*

Preheat the oven to 350° F.

Shred the zucchini through the large holes of a grater, then squeeze it firmly a handful at a time to extract much of the juice (which would make the dish watery if left in). Discard the juice, add it to a soup or sauce, or drink it. Toss the squeezed zucchini with the green onion and set aside. Stir together the flour, chili powder, and 1 teaspoon of salt and set aside.

Heat the butter in a skillet over moderate heat. Toss the chicken breasts in the flour mixture, shaking them so the excess flour falls off, then cook in the butter for about 3 to 4 minutes on each side, until lightly browned. Arrange the chicken in a single layer in a buttered casserole, and cover each with a mound of the zucchini mixture. Sprinkle lightly with salt and pepper, and cover with slices of cheese. Bake uncovered for about 20 minutes, until the cheese is lightly browned and the chicken is cooked through. Makes 4 servings.

3 medium zucchini
¼ cup chopped green onion
¼ cup flour
1 tablespoon chili powder
Salt
4 chicken breast halves, skinned and boned (but not pounded)
3 tablespoons butter
Freshly ground pepper
¼ pound jack cheese, thinly sliced

# Low-calorie Chicken and Artichoke Sauté

*Most of a chicken's fat lies in and under the skin, and once that's removed, the bird is relatively low in calories. This is a lovely sauté, with blanched baby artichokes and tarragon; the cooking juices reduce to a concentrated fat-free sauce, with just enough to moisten each serving. Serve with rice to catch the juices.*

5 or 6 baby artichokes (½ pound)
3 tablespoons olive oil
3½ to 4 pounds cut-up frying
   chicken, stripped of its skin
Salt and freshly ground pepper
½ cup chicken broth
½ cup dry white wine
2 teaspoons dried tarragon

Cut about 1 inch off the top of each artichoke, thus removing most of the prickly points. Quarter the artichokes, then with a small sharp knife, cut the tiny bit of hairy choke from the inside of each quarter. Drop the artichokes into a pot of boiling salted water and blanch for 5 minutes. Drain well and set aside.

Place the olive oil in a skillet over moderately high heat and brown the chicken pieces for about 5 minutes on each side, sprinkling lightly with salt and pepper. Remove the chicken from the pan for a moment and pour out the fat. Return the pan to heat and pour in the broth, wine, and tarragon. Bring to a boil, scraping all the browned bits from the bottom. Return the chicken and artichokes to the pan. Cover and simmer gently for about 20 minutes, basting two or three times with the liquid, until the chicken is cooked through. Remove the chicken and artichokes to a platter, raise heat to high, and boil until the sauce is reduced by about half. Spoon over the platter and sprinkle with parsley. Makes 4 or 5 servings.

# Chicken with Baked Pears

*I have been attracted to the flavor of chicken with pears ever since a French chef served me a version in which the pears were pureed with endive. This is a simplified version, with onions instead of endive.*

Slice the shallots or onions and boil them in the wine and stock until they are tender, about 10 minutes.

Meanwhile, peel and core the pears. Cut three of them in half and rub them with the cut lemon. Dice the remaining pear and squeeze some lemon juice over it to keep it from turning dark. Bone the chicken breasts and cut them in half.

Preheat the oven to 350° F.

Place the chicken breasts in a buttered baking pan. Season them lightly. Spread currant jelly on top of each one, then top each with a pear half, cut side down. Pour the shallot-enriched stock over the chicken and pears, add the diced pear, cover the pan, and bake for 30 minutes.

Remove the chicken breasts to a warm platter. Puree the liquid, along with the diced pears and the onions, to make a light sauce. Enrich it with cream, if you like. Taste for seasoning. Serve the chicken with the sauce, sprinkled with the chopped parsley or chives. Makes 6 servings.

2 shallots or 1 small onion
1 cup dry white wine
1 cup chicken stock
4 pears
1 lemon
3 whole chicken breasts
Salt and freshly ground pepper
2 tablespoons currant jelly
½ cup cream (optional)
¼ cup chopped parsley or chives (for garnish)

# Arroz con Pollo

*When I lived in Miami, this was my favorite dish to order at any of the city's many wonderful Cuban restaurants. I never tried to cook it myself until I settled in San Francisco and started missing it.*

**Basic recipe:**
1 chicken, about 3½ pounds
Salt and freshly ground pepper, paprika, and thyme
1 onion
2 cloves garlic
Pinch saffron threads
4 cups chicken stock or broth
2 cups uncooked long-grain white rice

**Optional ingredients:**
Bay leaf
½ cup dry white wine
2 pounds tomatoes, peeled, seeded and diced
½ cup frozen peas, defrosted
½ red bell pepper (or pimiento)

Cut the chicken into 8 pieces. Dice the onion, mash the garlic, and cut the bell pepper into thin strips (if included). Warm the stock in a saucepan.

Sauté the chicken in its own fat until light brown. Remove it to a 5-quart casserole. In the remaining fat in the pan, cook the onion and garlic until soft. Add 1 tablespoon oil if necessary.

Meanwhile, mash the saffron threads in a small cup with the back of a spoon and add them to the stock as it warms up.

When the onion is cooked, stir in the rice to coat it thoroughly. Stir in some of the stock (or the ½ cup dry white wine). Transfer the rice to the casserole with the rest of the stock. (Add the peas and bell peppers at this time, if you are using them.) Cover the casserole and bake it at 375° F. for 35 minutes. Makes 4 to 6 servings.

# Mushroom-stuffed Roast Chicken

*The chicken juices flavor the mushrooms while the thyme or marjoram-scented mushrooms return the favor. The main dish and the side dish cook together. A perfect opportunity to open a good Pinot Noir, although confirmed white wine drinkers will like a full-bodied Chardonnay.*

Preheat the oven to 375° F.

Remove the giblets and neck from the chicken, and rinse out the cavity. In a mixing bowl, toss the mushrooms with the seasonings. Stuff the chicken with the mixture. Close the chicken by overlapping the skin flaps at the vent, or skewer them shut with a toothpick, if you prefer.

Season the skin lightly with salt and pepper and place the chicken in a roasting pan. Roast it for 60 to 70 minutes, or until you can wiggle a leg in its socket.

Serve the chicken with the mushrooms. Makes 4 servings.

1 chicken (3¼ to 3½ pounds)
½ pound fresh white mushrooms, quartered
½ to 1 teaspoon leaf thyme or marjoram
½ teaspoon salt
Pinch freshly ground pepper

---

Q. *What can I use in place of wine in a recipe like veal scaloppine?*

A. Remember that the alcohol in wine burns off completely in a recipe like veal scaloppine, in which the wine is boiled rapidly to concentrate its flavor. So don't worry; there is no alcohol left in the finished dish. If you still don't want to use wine for one reason or another, you can substitute fruit juice, which will be sweeter, or better yet just use more broth or other flavorful liquid.

# Grilled Chicken Cayenne

*Easy to make, spicy hot, and because no fat is added, low in calories.*

2 broiler chickens (2½ to 3 pounds each), split
⅔ cup Dijon mustard or an herb mustard
1 to 2 tablespoons cayenne pepper
Salt

Build a large charcoal fire in your barbecue. Light it far enough in advance so that when you are ready to grill the chicken, the charcoal will have burned down to low-glowing embers.

Pat each chicken half dry with paper towels. Rub the skin sides with half the mustard, then dust with half the cayenne—the more you use, the hotter it will be. Place skin-side down on the grill, about 6 inches from glowing coals. Grill for about 15 minutes; use an atomizer or plant mister to douse any flare-ups.

While the chicken cooks, brush the top side with the remaining mustard and sprinkle with the remaining cayenne. Carefully turn the chicken—don't worry if a little of the mustard coating sticks to the grill. After 5 minutes, cover the grill, open the dampers fully, and cook 10 minutes. Remove the cover and cook 5 minutes more, turning the chicken once or twice if necessary, so it is evenly browned on both sides. Makes 4 servings.

# Glazed Chicken with Cucumber Sauce

*The cooling cucumber-yogurt sauce adds the right creamy touch to this Asian-influenced chicken sauté.*

Cut the cucumber in half lengthwise, scoop out the seeds, and chop it coarsely. Stir the cucumber and yogurt together and refrigerate until serving time. Heat the sesame oil in a skillet, and brown the chicken pieces for about 5 minutes on each side. Remove the chicken from the skillet, and pour out the browning fat. Add the soy and Worcestershire sauces, sugar, and water, scrape the bottom of the pan to loosen any browned bits, then return the chicken to the pan. Cover and cook for about 15 minutes, turning once. Uncover, turn up the heat, and boil until the liquid has reduced to a dark, syrupy glaze, turning the chicken several times. Arrange the chicken on a platter, and spoon some of the cucumber sauce over it. Pass the remaining sauce at the table. Makes 4 servings.

1 large cucumber
2 cups plain yogurt
3 tablespoons Oriental sesame oil
3 pounds cut-up frying chicken
2 tablespoons soy sauce
2 tablespoons Worcestershire sauce
2 tablespoons sugar
¼ cup water

# Baked Sesame Chicken

*The sesame flavor comes from two sources—the sesame oil brushed on the chicken and the sesame crackers that make the crust. To save on calories, skin the chicken first.*

4 boneless chicken breasts (8 half breasts)
1 teaspoon Oriental sesame oil
¼ cup sherry
¾ cup sour cream
1 cup crushed sesame crackers or 1 cup crushed saltines plus 1 teaspoon sesame seeds

Preheat the oven to 400° F.

Pat the chicken dry. Blend the oil and sherry, and use a brush to paint the chicken on both sides with the oil and sherry mixture. With a knife or spatula, spread both sides of the chicken with sour cream. Roll the chicken in cracker crumbs with sesame seeds. Place on a greased baking sheet. Bake for 25 to 30 minutes. Makes 4 large or 8 small servings.

# Chicken Sauté with Bourbon and Mushrooms

*A classic French chicken sauté with a twist—American bourbon in place of Cognac or brandy. The distinctive flavor of the liquor blends nicely.*

In a large, heavy skillet, heat the olive oil until it is almost smoking. Add the chicken pieces, season with salt and pepper, and brown well for about 5 minutes on each side. Drop the mushrooms over the chicken, reduce heat, and cover the skillet for about 5 minutes. Remove the cover and cook gently for about 5 minutes more. Remove the cooked chicken and mushrooms to a platter and keep warm.

Pour the cream into the skillet with the cooking juices, raise heat to high, and boil for about 3 to 5 minutes, until sauce has reduced by about a third and thickened slightly. It should coat the chicken pieces lightly. Season to taste with salt and pepper if necessary. Spoon over the chicken and mushrooms and sprinkle with the chopped parsley. Makes 4 servings.

**3 tablespoons olive oil**
**1 chicken (about 4 pounds), cut up**
**Salt and freshly ground pepper**
**½ pound mushrooms, quartered**
**⅓ cup bourbon**
**½ cup cream**
**2 tablespoons chopped parsley**

# Apricot-stuffed Chicken Thighs

*Chicken thighs are easy to bone—the one bone is easy to find. Just make a cut lengthwise on the meat side, and use your fingers to "scrape" the meat from the bone. Removing the bone leaves a hollow just begging to be stuffed.*

1 cup dried apricot halves
1 small onion, chopped
2 tablespoons butter
¼ cup chopped toasted almonds
½ teaspoon poultry seasoning
Salt and freshly ground pepper
8 chicken thighs, skinned and boned
2 tablespoons melted butter

Preheat the oven to 375° F.

Pour boiling water over the apricots and let them soak for several minutes to soften a little. Drain well and chop them fine, then place in a bowl. Cook the onion and butter together for about 5 minutes, until soft, then add to the apricots along with the almonds, poultry seasoning, and salt and pepper to taste.

Lay the chicken thighs flat and place about 2 tablespoons of filling on each one. Fold them in half lengthwise and skewer them closed with a toothpick. Arrange in a baking dish, brush with melted butter, sprinkle lightly with salt and pepper, then bake for about 35 to 40 minutes, until cooked through. Makes 4 servings.

# Deviled Chicken Legs

*In the never-ending search for an easy but different way to cook chicken for dinner, try this recipe. To separate the drumsticks from the thighs, turn the pieces skin side down and look for the line of yellowish fat that runs between the thigh and leg. Cut along the thigh side of that line— that's where the joint is.*

Preheat the oven to 375° F.

With a sharp knife, separate the legs from the thighs. Arrange the chicken pieces in a baking pan.

Combine the remaining ingredients, except for the bread crumbs, to made a marinade for the chicken. Pour it over the chicken, and let it marinate for 20 to 60 minutes. Roll the chicken in the marinade to coat it thoroughly and then in the bread crumbs. Drizzle remaining sauce over the chicken in the pan. Bake the chicken uncovered until it is golden brown, about 40 minutes. Makes 4 servings.

4 chicken legs and thighs (about 2½ pounds)
2 tablespoons Worcestershire sauce
2 tablespoons vegetable oil
2 tablespoons vermouth or red wine
1 teaspoon prepared mustard
½ teaspoon grated nutmeg
¾ cup fine bread crumbs

# Caramelized Squab

*On a visit to Dal Sole restaurant on Lake Maggiore, in Northern Italy, this was just one in a parade of sensational dishes. The use of raspberry vinegar and honey may seem "nouvelle," but squab has been prepared with them in Lombardy for generations.*

4 squabs
4 cloves garlic
Salt and freshly ground pepper
Fresh thyme
2 tablespoons olive oil
¼ cup honey
Oil for frying
1 tablespoon extra virgin olive oil
2 tablespoons raspberry vinegar

Rinse the squabs and pat dry. Split garlic cloves and rub the squabs all over. Sprinkle with salt, pepper, and chopped thyme. Rub with olive oil and honey. Marinate 30 minutes.

Preheat the oven to 450° F.

Put enough oil in a large skillet to film the bottom. Heat the pan and brown the squabs on all sides. Place the pan in the oven for 15 to 25 minutes, or until the squabs are done to your taste. Remove them from the pan. Carve the squabs for a fancy presentation, and serve with the pan sauce.

To make pan sauce, put pan on top of the stove. Add the oil and raspberry vinegar to the pan. Swirl to combine and spoon over the squabs. Serve with sautéed cabbage. Makes 4 servings.

Q. *My jar of honey seems to have developed a lot of crystals. Anything I can do about this?*

A. Crystals form in honey when it gets too cold. Warming the honey by placing the jar in a bowl of hot water should do the trick. You can also microwave it until the crystals dissolve.

# Low-calorie Turkey "Sauté"

*With the wide availability of turkey parts in supermarkets these days, this low-fat, easy-to-prepare dish is a snap to put together for a midweek dinner. Each generous serving contains less than 300 calories.*

Remove the skin from the turkey breast and slice the meat into pieces approximately ¼-inch thick, ¾-inch wide and 1½ inches long. Combine the strips in a bowl with the shallots, salt, pepper, nutmeg, and sherry.

Slice the mushrooms. In a large nonstick skillet, brown them in the butter, then add the chicken broth and turkey marinade. Let them simmer for 2 minutes. Add the turkey and the peas, and simmer the meat until it is opaque, about 3 minutes.

Dissolve the cornstarch in the milk, stirring with a teaspoon, then stir the mixture into the simmering stew. When it is thick, serve it with rice. Makes 4 generous servings.

**1 pound boneless turkey breast**
**1 large or 2 small shallots**
**Salt and freshly ground pepper**
**Pinch nutmeg**
**⅓ cup sherry**
**1 pound fresh mushrooms**
**1 tablespoon butter**
**2 cups chicken broth**
**1 cup frozen peas**
**2 tablespoons cornstarch**
**1 cup low-fat milk**

# Turkey Slices with Oranges

*A low-calorie way to reheat turkey, this recipe is also a good combination of flavors and colors. Serve with rice or boiled potatoes.*

1 tablespoon butter
3 large carrots, peeled and thinly
  sliced
3 ribs celery, thinly sliced
2 tablespoons chopped dill
4 oranges, preferably seedless
Salt and freshly ground pepper
1 pound (2 cups) sliced cooked turkey

Heat the butter in a large skillet, add the carrots and celery, then cover and cook gently for about 15 minutes, stirring or tossing occasionally. Grate on the zest of 1 orange, and sprinkle with the chopped dill. Season with salt and pepper.

Peel the oranges with a sharp knife, cutting away all the white pith. Now, working over a bowl to collect the juice, cut the orange segments from between the membranes. Pour whatever juice has collected into the skillet with the vegetables, place the turkey on top, then cover and cook gently for about 5 minutes. Scatter the orange segments over the turkey, cover, and cook about 2 minutes more. Don't cook it too long, or the turkey will dry out. Makes 4 servings.

# Turkey Meat Loaf

*Eleanor Radanovich won the "KCBS Kitchen"/Max's Diner meat-loaf cooking contest with this excellent variation. Serve it in the fall when thoughts are turning to turkey and the traditional trimmings.*

Preheat the oven to 350° F.

Assemble all ingredients and put the meat in a large mixing bowl. Ground meat is easier to handle at room temperature. Mix all the ingredients but the bacon together thoroughly with your hands. Form a roll and place it in a shallow baking pan. Lay bacon strips on top of the loaf. Bake for 1 hour. Remove from oven and allow to cool slightly before slicing.

Serving suggestion: Place the loaf on a heated serving platter surrounded by cooked carrots, potatoes, and broccoli flowerets. Serve with cranberry sauce. Makes 8 servings.

2 pounds ground turkey
1 cup bread cubes or stuffing mix
1 medium onion, finely chopped
1 large apple, cored, peeled, and chopped
¾ cup chopped celery
¼ cup broken or chopped walnuts (optional)
¼ cup raisins (optional)
2 eggs beaten with 2 tablespoons milk
1 teaspoon poultry seasoning
1 teaspoon salt
½ teaspoon freshly ground pepper
2 strips bacon

# Turkey Mushroom Patties

*Low-fat, low-calorie ground turkey can also be low-flavor and dry unless you dress it up. The soaked bread crumbs take care of the texture and mushrooms deepen the flavor. Serve these patties on a bun with the usual hamburger trimmings, and try some Hot Cabbage and Pepper Slaw (page 172) on the side.*

2 pounds ground turkey
2 cups chopped fresh mushrooms
½ cup dry bread crumbs soaked in ¼ cup milk
¼ cup finely chopped onions
¼ cup finely chopped celery
2 teaspoons Dijon mustard
2 teaspoons leaf thyme
3 eggs
Olive oil or vegetable oil

Combine all the ingredients except the eggs and oil. Beat the eggs until they are very light; mix them into the other ingredients. With wet hands, shape the mixture into patties.

Film the bottom of a large skillet with oil, and set over moderately high heat until oil is almost smoking. Place the patties in the pan, and fry for about 3 minutes per side, until cooked through and the meat is no longer pink in the center. Reduce heat if they are browning too quickly. Serve hot from the pan. Makes about 16 small patties, 2 per serving.

# Turkey Chutney Burgers

*Another way to dress up ground turkey. Use any type of chutney. It doesn't always have to be mango.*

C ombine all the ingredients except the oil in a mixing bowl. Beat mixture gently with a fork until thoroughly combined. Shape into 4 patties, each about 1 inch thick and 4 inches across.

Film the bottom of a large skillet with oil, and set over moderately high heat until oil is almost smoking. Place the burgers in the pan, and fry for about 6 to 7 minutes a side, until cooked through and the meat is no longer pink in the center. Reduce heat if burgers are browning too quickly. Serve hot from the pan, with lots of chilled yogurt and a green salad. Makes 4 servings.

1½ pounds ground turkey
4 teaspoons curry powder
½ teaspoon salt
½ teaspoon freshly ground pepper
½ cup chutney (finely chopped if it has large pieces)
Dash Tabasco
Olive oil or vegetable oil

LOW CALORIE · LOW FAT ·

# Anchovy-kissed Turkey Burgers

*Tubes of anchovy paste are readily available, and they keep nicely in the refrigerator. The flavor adds a welcome touch to liven up homey fare such as this low-calorie family supper item.*

1 pound ground turkey
½ teaspoon salt
½ teaspoon freshly ground pepper
2 tablespoons vegetable oil
½ cup chicken broth
½ cup dry white wine
1 teaspoon anchovy paste
1 tablespoon capers
1 tablespoon butter

Season the turkey with the salt and pepper. Shape it into 4 patties about 3 inches across and 1 inch thick. Heat the oil in a skillet and cook the turkey burgers for about 5 minutes on each side, until cooked through but not dried out. Remove from the pan and keep them warm for a few minutes.

Pour in broth and wine in the skillet and boil over high heat, scraping the bottom of the pan, until the liquid is reduced by half. Add the anchovy paste, capers, and butter, stir until blended, and taste; add salt and pepper if necessary. Spoon the sauce over the burgers. Makes 4 servings.

# STUFFING

Every November, I try to come up with a few new ideas for stuffing the holiday turkey. Here are some of my favorites, all of which are perfectly suitable for chicken or duck, if you prefer:

# Jalapeño Corn Bread Dressing

Crumble corn bread into a large bowl. Add bread cubes. Brown the sausage along with the onions and celery. When the sausage loses its red color, drain off all but about ¼ cup of the fat. Add the salt, thyme, sage, and jalapeño peppers. Combine with the bread mixture. Blend the broth with the eggs. Mix well and add this to the stuffing to moisten it. Spoon it lightly into the turkey cavities. Makes enough for 12- to 15-pound turkey. Or bake it separately in a 3-quart casserole, basting it with the drippings from the turkey.

1 corn bread (page 117)
6 cups dry bread cubes
1 pound bulk sausage (mild)
1 cup chopped onion
1½ cups chopped celery
1½ teaspoons salt
½ teaspoon dried thyme
½ teaspoon rubbed sage
¼ cup chopped, seeded jalapeño peppers
1 cup turkey giblet broth or chicken broth
2 eggs

# Kernel Corn and Corn Bread Stuffing

1 corn bread, your favorite recipe or
  mine (page 117)
1 pound pork sausage (or, for a
  spicier version, chorizo)
1 onion, chopped
1 green bell pepper, seeded and
  chopped
1 or 2 mild chilies, seeded and
  chopped
2 ribs celery, chopped
2 cups whole-kernel corn, fresh,
  frozen, or canned
Chopped parsley
5 cups dry bread cubes

While the corn bread is baking, brown and crumble the sausage in a large skillet. Add the onion, pepper, chilies, and celery. Cook them until they are soft. Drain off any extra fat, and put the sausage mixture in a large mixing bowl. Crumble the corn bread into the mixture, along with the corn, some chopped parsley (or cilantro), and the bread cubes. If the mixture seems too dry, moisten with white wine.

Makes enough to stuff a 14- to 16-pound turkey.

# Corn Bread and Chard Stuffing

1 onion, chopped
6 tablespoons (¾ stick) butter (or
  bacon drippings, or a combination)
1 corn bread (page 117)
½ cup fried, crumbled bacon (about
  4 strips)
1½ cups chopped cooked Swiss
  chard (2 bunches)
2 teaspoons poultry seasoning
Salt and freshly ground pepper
Chicken stock

Cook the onion in the butter for about 5 minutes, until softened; set aside.

Crumble the corn bread into a large bowl, and toss together with the bacon, chard, poultry seasoning, and cooked onion. Taste and correct seasoning with salt and pepper. It won't need much salt, especially if the corn bread was salted. If the stuffing seems dry, toss in about ¼ to ½ cup of chicken stock. Makes enough for a 12- to 15-pound turkey.

# Rice Stuffing with Dates

Rinse the rice well and combine it in a 3-quart saucepan with the water or stock and 2 teaspoons of the salt. Bring the rice to a boil, cover the pan, lower the heat, and cook the rice over very low heat for 18 minutes, or until the water is absorbed.

Meanwhile, dice the onion and celery, and sauté them gently in butter until they are soft. Cut the sausage into ¼-inch slices; cut large sausages in halves or quarters first so the pieces will be small enough. Coarsely chop the dates. Chop the cilantro leaves and thinly slice the green onions.

When the rice is cooked, turn it into a large bowl and let it cool before combining it with the prepared ingredients, remaining 1 teaspoon salt, pepper, and the eggs lightly beaten with the milk. Makes enough for a 12- to 15-pound turkey.

3 ½ cups uncooked pearl rice
5 cups water or stock or part stock
3 teaspoons salt
2 medium onions
⅓ stalk celery, chopped (about 1 ½ cups)
4 tablespoons (½ stick) butter
12 ounces Chinese sausage or other cooked sausage
12 ounces pitted dates
⅓ cup cilantro leaves
2 or 3 green onions
8 ounces water chestnuts, coarsely chopped (optional)
¼ teaspoon freshly ground pepper
3 eggs
¾ cup milk

# Fennel-Walnut Stuffing

8 cups dry bread cubes
1 medium onion
1 large bulb fennel (sweet anise)
¾ pound fresh mushrooms
1 pound bulk sausage, mild (preferably your own)
8 ounces walnut meats, chopped (about 1½ cups)
1½ teaspoons salt
1 teaspoon dried thyme
1 teaspoon rubbed sage
¼ cup finely chopped parsley
1 cup chicken or turkey-giblet broth
2 eggs

Place the bread cubes in a large bowl. Chop the onion, fennel, and mushrooms.

Brown the sausage along with the onion and fennel. When the sausage loses its color and the fennel is soft, remove the ingredients with a slotted spoon and drain off all but about 3 tablespoons of the fat. Add the mushrooms to the pan, and brown them lightly, adding the walnuts for the last few minutes. Add the cooked ingredients to the bread cubes, along with the salt, thyme, sage, and parsley.

Combine the broth and eggs. Mix this well and use it to moisten the stuffing. Spoon it lightly into the turkey cavities. Makes enough for a 15-pound turkey.

**Q.** *My mother used to roast her turkey in a paper bag, so she didn't have to baste it. Is it just as good to wrap it in foil? Or is there a better way?*

**A.** My mother used to roast her chickens and turkeys in paper bags, too, but that was before recycled paper was so common. The chemicals used in the recycling process are not the sort of thing you want in your food. Foil is not a good substitute. Paper is more porous than foil. In foil, chicken or turkey essentially steams.

I recommend roasting chicken or turkey uncovered. And don't baste it. Why baste? It just flavors the skin, which nobody wants to eat anymore, and slows down the roasting process because every time you open the door to baste, the oven temperature drops 50 to 75 degrees. Season the skin, rub it with butter or oil, put it in the oven, and ignore it until you are ready to check to see if the bird is done.

# CHAPTER THREE:

# GRAINS

# GRAINS

Grains are the foods of the hour. You would have to be living on another planet to have avoided the hype over the benefits of fiber on one's cholesterol count, particularly if the fiber should happen to be oat bran. But the benefits of eating grains go beyond the hype. Not only are grains delicious—who doesn't love a dinner of pasta or polenta?—but nutritionists also tell us we should eat more of them because a diet high in grains tends to be a diet low in fat. When I eat more bread than meat at dinner, or center a whole meal around pasta or rice, I get up from the table pleasantly full, but not overwhelmed.

From the cook's standpoint, grain dishes have other advantages. Cooking techniques are not difficult, and for the most part grains are not very expensive to prepare. Many pasta and rice dishes cook quickly, and they have the added attraction of being great absorbers of leftovers. My family has enjoyed many a delicious dinner of polenta, a few slices of cooked chicken, turkey, or beef, and a topping of marinara sauce and freshly grated Parmesan cheese. The polenta takes 10 minutes to prepare and the rest is just reheating. Want to make it fancier? Try the Baked Polenta and Prawns (page 137), which turns a plebeian dish into a feast.

Grains are simple food. Most of the peoples of the world make them the staples of their diets. Yet grains seem to cause a great deal of confusion among many cooks. To help sort out the details, here is a brief guide:

## RICE

The basic process is to use 2 cups of water to 1 cup of white rice, bring it to a boil, cover the pan, lower the heat to the barest simmer, and leave it alone for 18 minutes. Salt, pepper and butter to taste. Having fielded many questions from listeners trying to calculate how much rice to start with to come out with the right number of servings, I offer the following rule for those with the same problem: Divide the number of servings you want by two to get the number of cups of cooked rice, then divide that by three to get the number of cups of raw rice to use. Add twice as much water and proceed. For firmer rice, use less water, as little as 1½ cups per cup of rice. Timing remains the same.

Other forms of rice can be confusing. Charts in cookbooks offer a variety of cooking times and amounts of water to use for brown rice, wild rice, etc. A chef acquaintance taught me the easiest solution: Treat wild rice or brown rice like pasta. Put it in a large pot of boiling water and cook it until it is as tender as you like. (Brown rice will take about 30 minutes, wild rice about 40.)

# PASTA

I used to make fresh pasta with semolina flour, having heard that all good pasta is made with the hard wheat flour to give it the right bite. It took a terrific Italian cook to set me straight. Home-made fresh pasta is supposed to be tender. Dry pasta is supposed to have the "right bite."

Fresh homemade pasta is best when made the old-fashioned way, blending the eggs and flour by hand, rolling it out in a hand-cranked (or motor-driven) pasta machine, then cooked quickly just before serving. Making the pasta in a food processor is quite a bit faster, and you would have to be an expert to tell the difference. The trick in the food processor is to mix all the ingredients at once with the metal blade, but don't add enough liquid for it to form a ball or it will be too sticky. It should form a kind of a coarse-grained meal, which will form a dough when pressed together. One of the big advantages of making your own pasta is you can add your own flavors to it. See the recipes for Red Pepper Pasta (page 134) and Garlic Parmesan Noodles (page 135).

Dry pasta is easier. All you need to do is boil it in lots of salted water, allowing at least 1 quart per 2 ounces of pasta. Be sure to use enough water. The prime cause of gummy pasta is boiling it in too little water. Boil it enough so that it is cooked through but still firm (not crunchy). A tablespoon or two of olive oil added to the boiling water will help keep the pasta from sticking together as it cooks. Never rinse pasta unless you're going to serve it cold in a salad. Figure on six servings per pound of dry pasta.

# BREAD, BISCUITS, AND MUFFINS

Homemade bread doesn't have to mean hours-to-prepare yeast bread, delicious and heartwarming as it may be. Little breads, such as biscuits and muffins, are easier to make quickly and often more interesting. The muffins in this chapter, for example, are flavored with such diverse things as currants, curry, peanut butter, cranberries, and pumpkins. Biscuits can take creative flavorings, too. Consider my Sage-Pepper Biscuits (page 109) or Coconut Biscuits (page 111) for examples.

Bread secrets are not difficult. Basically, be sure to knead yeast breads enough, but mix muffins and biscuits as little as possible. Everything else is extra credit. For example, those who want to make yeast breads with limited time have two options. To speed up the process, 8 minutes in a covered bowl on the lowest setting (10 percent power) of a microwave oven will generate enough warmth to get a two-loaf recipe to complete its first rising in 15 to 20 minutes. Alternately, you can make the dough and put it in the refrigerator, which will slow down the rising enough that a normal one-hour first rise will take eight to ten. A busy person can use this technique to start a loaf in the morning and finish it in the evening.

# Apple-Cinnamon Muffins with Oat Bran

*Frozen apple juice concentrate provides all the sweetening these muffins need, and the addition of chopped apple adds great texture.*

2 ¼ cups oat bran
2 teaspoons apple pie spice
1 tablespoon baking powder
½ cup milk
¾ cup (6 ounces) frozen apple juice
   concentrate
1 egg
2 tablespoons vegetable oil
1 medium apple, chopped (don't peel
   it)
⅓ cup raisins

Preheat the oven to 425° F.

Mix the dry ingredients in a large bowl. Mix together the milk, apple juice, egg, oil, apple, and raisins, and stir into the dry ingredients.

Spoon the mixture into muffin tins lined with fluted paper baking cups, filling each about two-thirds full. Bake for 16 to 17 minutes. Cool on a rack. Store these in a plastic bag or a covered bowl. Makes 12 muffins.

---

Q. *What is the difference between oat bran and oatmeal?*

A. Oat bran is the fiber in the hull of the grain. It has no vitamins, just fiber. Oatmeal contains some oat bran but also the rest of the whole grain. In cooking, they are not interchangeable, although oat bran can make an excellent muffin without flour.

# Cranberry Muffins

*A not-too-sweet muffin, flecked with red, with a delicate cranberry and orange flavor. A food processor is the easiest way to chop cranberries. These muffins are good warm, with a meal, and leftovers are delicious for breakfast, split, toasted, and buttered.*

Preheat the oven to 400° F.

Either butter muffin tins or line them with cupcake papers.

In a small bowl, stir and toss together the flour, baking powder, baking soda, salt, and sugar. In a larger bowl, beat the eggs, milk, butter, orange zest, and cranberries. Add the combined dry ingredients and beat just until blended. Spoon the batter into prepared muffin tins, filling each cup about two-thirds full. Bake for about 15 minutes, or until a toothpick inserted in the center of a muffin comes out clean. Makes about 16 muffins.

1½ cups flour
1½ teaspoons baking powder
½ teaspoon baking soda
¼ teaspoon salt
¼ cup sugar
2 eggs
⅔ cup milk
5⅓ tablespoons (⅔ stick) melted butter
Grated zest of 1 orange
1 cup finely chopped cranberries

# Pumpkin Muffins

*The very first recipe ever given on the "KCBS Kitchen," the day we went on the air, March 1, 1982. I had just returned from a conference at the Greenbrier resort hotel, White Sulphur Springs, West Virginia, where I fell in love with these sweet, almost candied mini-muffins served at breakfast. The chef was pleased to share the recipe.*

½ cup (1 stick) butter, softened

1 cup sugar

1¼ cups mashed pumpkin or pumpkin puree

2 large eggs

1½ cups flour

1 teaspoon cinnamon

¼ teaspoon freshly grated nutmeg

2 teaspoons baking powder

1 cup milk

¼ cup finely chopped walnuts (optional)

½ cup raisins (optional)

Preheat the oven to 400° F.

Grease muffin tins, 12 medium ones or 3 to 4 dozen small ones; the small ones are preferred. In a large bowl, cream the butter with the sugar and the pumpkin. Blend in the eggs.

In another bowl, sift together the flour, cinnamon, nutmeg, and baking powder. Gently mix the dry ingredients into the pumpkin mixture, alternating with the milk, stirring the mixture just long enough to incorporate all the ingredients. Fold in the walnuts and raisins.

Spoon the batter into muffin tins. Sprinkle the tops with additional cinnamon and sugar, if you like. Bake for 25 minutes (small tins), 35 to 40 minutes (large tins), or until they are nicely browned on top. Remove the muffins from the tins onto wire racks to cool. These are delicious the second day, and they freeze well. Makes 12 regular or 3 to 4 dozen small muffins.

# Curried Pumpkin Muffins

*Not breakfast muffins, but these are just the things to serve with a fruit salad at lunch or dinner or for a snack.*

Preheat the oven to 400° F.

Grease muffin tins or line them with fluted paper baking cups.

Combine the butter and sugar in a mixing bowl, and beat until blended. Add the pumpkin and eggs and beat until completely mixed. The mixture will look curdled, which is OK. In another bowl, stir and toss together the flour, salt, baking powder, and curry powder. Add the combined dry ingredients to the creamed mixture, and beat just until the batter is combined—it will be thick.

Spoon into the muffin tins, filling each cup about two-thirds full. Bake for about 20 minutes, or until a toothpick inserted in the center of a muffin comes out clean. Makes 12 muffins.

4 tablespoons (½ stick) soft butter
½ cup brown sugar
1 cup mashed, cooked pumpkin, fresh or canned
2 eggs
1½ cups flour
½ teaspoon salt
2 teaspoons baking powder
2 teaspoons curry powder

# Lemon and Poppy Seed Muffins

*One of my favorite breakfast muffins, these have a refreshing tartness accented by sour cream.*

1¾ cups flour
1 teaspoon baking powder
½ teaspoon baking soda
⅓ cup sugar
2 tablespoons poppy seeds
1 lemon
1 cup sour cream
1 extra-large egg
2 tablespoons milk

Preheat the oven to 400°.

Butter the muffin pans or line them with fluted paper baking cups.

In a mixing bowl, sift together the dry ingredients. Grate the lemon zest onto a piece of wax paper, and stir it into the dry ingredients. Squeeze the juice from the lemon into a small bowl, and blend in the sour cream, egg, and milk. Fold this mixture into the dry ingredients until they are just combined. Spoon into muffin pans.

Bake for 20 to 25 minutes, until they are lightly browned and test done when pierced with a clean knife. Makes 8 or 9 muffins.

Q. *I have a recipe that calls for superfine sugar, but all I have is regular granulated sugar. Can I use it?*

A. Superfine sugar is just granulated sugar ground into finer crystals so it will dissolve more quickly. You can achieve the same effect by processing regular granulated sugar in a food processor for 30 to 45 seconds.

# Sage-Pepper Biscuits

*These small biscuits make a delicious hors d'oeuvre, split and topped with a dab of mustard or mayonnaise and a piece of country ham or smoked meat. The full amount of pepper makes them quite spicy; use less if you want a milder flavor.*

Preheat the oven to 425° F.

Stir together the dry ingredients. Drop in the shortening and blend it into the dry ingredients with a pastry blender or your fingers. Add the buttermilk and stir until the dough holds together. Turn it onto a lightly floured surface and knead about 12 times. Pat the dough to a thickness of ½ inch. Cut biscuits with a 1½-inch round cutter. Place the biscuits, barely touching, on a greased baking sheet, and bake for about 12 to 15 minutes, until puffy and lightly browned. Makes about 30 small biscuits.

1½ cups flour
½ cup cornmeal
½ teaspoon salt
2 teaspoons baking powder
½ teaspoon baking soda
1 to 2 teaspoons freshly ground pepper
2 teaspoons dried sage
⅓ cup vegetable shortening
⅔ cup buttermilk

# Mayonnaise Biscuits

*Mayonnaise is mostly oil, and with its creamy texture it cuts into a dough more easily than butter. Use a good quality one—the cheap oil flavor in inexpensive mayonnaise will haunt the biscuits. If you make your own olive oil mayonnaise, these are especially good.*

2 cups flour
4 teaspoons baking powder
1 tablespoon sugar
¼ teaspoon salt
½ cup mayonnaise
½ cup plus 1 or 2 tablespoons milk

Preheat the oven to 450° F.

Stir and toss together the dry ingredients. In a separate bowl, whisk together the mayonnaise and ½ cup of the milk. Pour over the dry ingredients and stir until the mixture forms a cohesive mass. The dough should feel soft and satiny; if it seems dry, add another tablespoon or 2 of milk and stir.

Turn the dough out onto a lightly floured surface, and knead gently about 8 times. Pat into a 5 × 8-inch rectangle about ½-inch thick. With a sharp knife, cut the dough into 12 squares by making two cuts lengthwise and three across. Place them, just touching one another, on an ungreased baking sheet. Bake for about 15 minutes, until puffy and light brown. Serve piping hot. Makes 12 biscuits.

# Coconut Biscuits

*The subtle flavor of coconut milk not only gives these batter biscuits a delicious flavor but the texture takes a subtle turn toward smooth as well. The cake flour makes it especially smooth.*

Preheat the oven to 400° F. Grease a 12-cup muffin tin.

Combine ingredients in a food processor and pulse four or five times. *Do not overmix*. Texture will be like that of chocolate-chip cookie dough. Spoon into muffin cups and bake for 25 minutes. For mini-biscuit size, bake for 18 to 20 minutes.

If you do not use a food processor, mix the dry ingredients well, then cut in the butter or shortening. Quickly stir in the coconut milk and milk. *Do not overmix*. Makes 12 regular biscuits.

3 cups cake flour
¼ cup sugar
1½ tablespoons baking powder
1 teaspoon salt
½ cup (1 stick) butter or ¼ cup butter, ¼ cup shortening
1 cup coconut milk or coconut juice
2 tablespoons milk or buttermilk

# Oat Bran Biscotti

*OK, so this is not the most nutritious way to get your fiber, but the texture the bran contributes makes these cookies especially good.*

1⅓ cups (6 ounces) toasted almonds
1½ cups flour
1½ cups oat bran
⅔ cup sugar
1 teaspoon baking powder
¼ teaspoon salt
4 tablespoons (½ stick) butter at
   room temperature
2 eggs

Preheat the oven to 325° F.

Generously butter a 9 × 13-inch baking dish or, if you have them, three metal ice cube trays (about 4 × 10 inches each, with the inserts removed).

In a food processor, pulverize half of the toasted almonds to a fine powder, and dump them in a large bowl. Coarsely chop the remaining almonds with several on-off pulses and add them to the bowl. Add the dry ingredinets to the nuts and toss to combine thoroughly. Drop in the butter and blend until thoroughly incorporated—your hands are the best tools for this job. Add the eggs and blend until the dough holds together; it will be very stiff and a little crumbly. If necessary, add a tablespoon or two of water.

Press the dough evenly in the prepared pan or among the ice cube trays and bake for about 30 minutes, until lightly browned around the edges. Remove from the oven, let cool a few minutes, and then, with a sharp knife, cut into 1 × 3-inch rectangles. Carefully lift from the pan and place the cookies on their sides on an ungreased baking sheet. Return to the oven for about 15 minutes more, until golden. Store airtight.

These cookies are good for dipping in coffee or hot chocolate, and because they are less sweet than most biscotti, they are very good served with a bowl of sliced fresh fruit for breakfast or a mid-morning snack. Makes about 30 cookies.

# Scones

*When John Tovey, chef and owner of Miller Howe Inn, Lake Winder-
mere, England, visited San Francisco to cook for a week at a hotel, he
also visited the "KCBS Kitchen" and shared his secret for the tenderest,
lightest scones imaginable. Tovey recommends patting the dough out into
a rectangle and cutting diamond shapes to use it all without rerolling.
"Do not roll the mixture out and cut it into delightful scalloped circles and
then economically reroll to get a few more," he says. "If you do, your
scones are bound to be heavier."*

Preheat the oven to 425° F.
Sift together the flour, baking powder, and salt into a large mixing bowl.
Divide the soft butter into pieces of about 2 tablespoons and scatter them over
the flour mixture. Now here's the trick for the lightest scones. Don't dig in
and pinch the butter and flour together as if you were making biscuits. Scoop up
a handful of flour and butter and very, very lightly run your thumb across your
fingers, allowing the flour to sift through your fingers. At first, it will seem as if
nothing is happening, but within 2 minutes the mixture will resemble fine
crumbs.

Now add the sugar, raisins, and eggs. Gently fold them into the flour mixture
as if you were mixing a soufflé. Keep it light. Hands are the best tool for this.

It is virtually impossible to tell you exactly how much milk to use. It depends
on how soft the butter is, how warm the room is, and other variables. But start
with about ½ cup, and add a bit more at a time, folding and mixing to make a
soft dough. This is a good place to use up that last bit of sour cream or half-and-
half, too.

Turn the dough out onto a lightly floured board. Do not knead it. Just pat it
into a large rectangle about an inch thick. Cut it into diamond shapes about 2½
or 3 inches long and 1½ inches wide.

Put the diamonds on 2 lightly greased baking sheets. Bake them at 425° F. for
10 minutes, or until they are lightly browned and puffed. Makes 36 to 40
scones.

You can make savory scones out of the same recipe by omitting the sugar and
raisins and by using ½ cup grated cheese and a teaspoon of ground coriander or
curry powder.

4 cups flour
2 tablespoons baking powder
2 teaspoons salt
1½ cups (3 sticks) butter, very soft
6 tablespoons sugar
½ cup golden raisins
4 eggs, lightly beaten
About 1 cup milk or sour cream

# Light Oatmeal Pancakes

*These pancakes will appeal to those who like whole grains and health foods, but they are so light that you don't have to be nutrition-conscious to like them.*

1 cup drained cooked or canned
   white beans
½ cup uncooked oatmeal
2 eggs
⅓ cup honey
½ cup milk
½ cup whole-wheat flour
1 ½ teaspoons baking powder
½ teaspoon baking soda

In a blender or food processor, combine the oatmeal and beans; process until both are thoroughly combined and finely chopped. Add the eggs, honey, and milk, and process again until blended.

In a medium bowl, stir and toss together the flour, baking powder, and baking soda. (These really don't seem to need salt, but you could add a pinch now if you wish.) Add the bean mixture, and stir with a fork just until blended—a few small lumps in the batter are okay.

Drop by heaping tablespoons onto a hot greased griddle. In a minute or so, when the edges are set and the top full of bubbles, turn and brown the other side. Makes about 20 4-inch cakes. These are especially good with maple syrup.

# Whole-wheat Sesame Crackers

*Homemade crackers are so unusual that your friends and family are bound to be impressed. More important, these are delicious with all kinds of drinks, dips, salads, and cheeses. They last for weeks.*

In a bowl, combine the dry ingredients and the sesame seeds. Cut in the butter. (If you do this in a food processor, cut the butter in with short bursts, just until it forms a mixture like cornmeal.)

Blend in the milk. In a food processor, pour in the milk and incorporate with several short bursts. The mixture should not form a ball, but should hold together when pressed in clumps.

Preheat the oven to 425° F.

Divide the dough in half and form it into a square. Roll it out on a floured board into a rectangle about 1/16-inch thick. The rectangles will be about 10 × 12 inches. Place this rectangle on an ungreased baking sheet. Score the edge and in roughly 2-inch intervals, forming a crosshatch pattern, not cutting through the pastry but leaving a deep mark in it. (A ravioli wheel is a good tool to use for this, but a fork will do.)

Bake the dough for 6 minutes, or until the edges begin to turn a golden brown. Turn the dough with a spatula and bake for 5 minutes. The edge should be very brown. The edges and the crackers will snap off easily when they are cool. Repeat with the remaining dough.

Cool the crackers on a wire rack while you prepare and bake the rest of the dough. Makes 32 to 40 crackers.

1 cup white flour
1 cup whole-wheat flour
½ teaspoon salt
1 teaspoon sesame seeds
¼ cup (½ stick) butter
⅔ cup milk

# Crispy Cheese Wafers

*These make a great snack, or you can serve them in place of bread with soup or salad.*

1 generous cup shredded or finely
    cubed Cheddar (about ¼ pound)
½ cup shortening
¼ teaspoon salt
Several drops Tabasco
1½ cups flour
2 tablespoons Dijon or yellow
    mustard

Fit the food processor with the shredding disk and grate the cheese. With the cheese still in the bowl, put in the steel blade and process the shortening and cheese until smooth. Add the salt and Tabasco and process again until smooth. Add the flour and mustard; process until the dough forms a ball that whirls around the blade.

Lacking a food processor, shred the cheese and cream it with the shortening, then knead in the remaining ingredients to make a smooth dough.

Turn out onto a lightly floured surface, and push and pat into a log about 9 inches long and 1½ to 2 inches across. Wrap in wax paper or plastic wrap, and chill until firm—at least 2 hours or up to several days.

When ready to bake, preheat the oven to 400° F.

With a thin, sharp knife, cut the chilled cheese roll into slices about ¼-inch thick. Place 1 inch apart on an ungreased baking sheet, and bake for about 10 minutes, until lightly browned and slightly puffy. Transfer to racks to cool. Makes about 40.

The unbaked dough keeps well in the refrigerator in log form, and the baked wafers remain fresh for at least a week if stored airtight.

# Harvey's Corn Bread

*Baking this in a skillet, preferably an old black cast-iron skillet, is the trick to giving the crust the right crisp texture.*

Preheat the oven to 400° F. Grease an 8-inch skillet.

Sift together the dry ingredients except cornmeal. (Even if you don't like sweet corn bread, use at least the minimum amount of sugar. It won't be too sweet.) Stir in the cornmeal. In a measuring cup or small bowl, beat together the milk and eggs until they are smooth. Stir them into the corn mixture just until the ingredients are moistened. Stir in the butter. Pour and scrape the batter into the skillet.

Bake for 25 to 30 minutes, just until the top is lightly browned. Serve hot, cut into 8 to 10 wedges.

1 cup sifted flour
1 tablespoon baking powder
1 teaspoon salt
1 to 2 tablespoons sugar
1 cup cornmeal
2 eggs
1 cup milk
4 tablespoons (¼ cup) melted butter

# Whole-wheat Irish Soda Bread

*The usual recipe you see for Irish soda bread resembles a sweet muffin or scone. This bread is more like you would find in County Bannock. I like to toast thin slices for breakfast.*

2½ cups whole-wheat flour
1½ cups white flour
2 teaspoons salt
1 teaspoon baking soda
¾ teaspoon baking powder
1½ to 2 cups buttermilk

Preheat the oven to 375° F.

Grease an 8-inch cake pan or a baking sheet.

Sift the dry ingredients together to distribute the baking soda and baking powder. Add enough buttermilk to make a soft dough. If you don't have buttermilk, sour 2 cups of milk by mixing it with 2 tablespoons vinegar or lemon juice. Turn the dough out onto a floured board, and knead it 2 or 3 minutes, or until it feels smooth and velvety.

Shape the dough into a round loaf, and set it in a well-buttered 8-inch cake pan or on a well-buttered cookie sheet. With a sharp knife dipped in flour, cut a broad "X" ½ inch into the top of the loaf. This is traditional in soda breads; it spreads open as the bread bakes to make an attractive shape.

Bake for 35 to 40 minutes, or until the loaf sounds hollow when tapped on the bottom. This is especially delicious the next day, sliced very thin, toasted, and served with sweet butter and marmalade.

# Baked Bean Bread

*This moist, brownish-blond quick bread with the subtle flavor of baked beans makes a good choice to serve with ham or with roast or grilled chicken.*

Preheat the oven to 350° F.

Grease and flour two 8 × 4 × 2 ½-inch loaf pans.

In a medium-size mixing bowl, stir and toss together the flour, salt, baking powder, and baking soda until completely blended; set aside.

Puree the beans in a food mill or a food processor. In another bowl, place the bean puree, shortening, eggs, brown sugar, and milk. Beat with a whisk or hand-held electric mixer until thoroughly mixed. (Some tiny lumps of shortening left in the mixture are okay.) Add the combined dry ingredients and beat just until batter is blended.

Spread evenly in the prepared pans, and bake for about 50 minutes, or until a thin wood skewer or toothpick inserted in the center of a loaf comes out clean. Makes 2 loaves.

2 ½ cups flour
1 teaspoon salt
2 teaspoons baking powder
1 teaspoon baking soda
2 cups baked beans
⅓ cup vegetable shortening
4 eggs
½ cup brown sugar
½ cup milk

Q. *I have a quick bread that calls for a 9 × 5 × 4-inch loaf pan. If I make the loaf in 7 × 3 × 3-inch pans, how do I figure out how many pans and how much batter to make?*

A. Remember junior high-school geometry? Multiply the width times the height and depth to get the volume of a container. So the 9-inch pan comes out to 180 cubic inches and the 7-inch pan comes out to 63 inches. The batter for your 9-inch pan will fill about three of the smaller ones.

# Italian Whole-wheat Loaves

*Years ago, I had lunch with a friend in an old-time Italian restaurant in New York. The lunch was not memorable, but the bread was. When I got home I worked out this recipe, which comes very close.*

3 to 3 ½ cups white flour
3 cups whole-wheat flour
2 packages active dry yeast
2 cups water
1 tablespoon sugar
2 teaspoons salt
2 tablespoons olive oil

Stir 2 cups of the white flour with yeast in a large bowl. In a saucepan, heat water, sugar, and salt until warm to the touch (120° to 130° F.). Add to flour and yeast with the shortening and beat with an electric mixer at high speed for 3 minutes. The batter should be smooth.

Add the whole-wheat flour and enough additional white flour to form a rough mass that pulls away from the sides of the bowl. Turn out onto a floured surface and knead until smooth, 10 to 13 minutes, or use a heavy-duty mixer with a dough hook. Cover the dough with a bowl and let it rise until it is double in bulk (about 45 to 55 minutes).

Punch down the dough. Divide it into three parts of equal size. Form each of them into a loaf about 13 inches long, or shorter, stubbier loaves if you prefer.

Sprinkle a baking sheet with cornmeal. Place loaves on the sheet, make several diagonal slices on top with a very sharp knife, and cover the loaves with a towel. Place them in a cold oven on the middle rack, and place a pan of boiling water on the lower rack. Let rise 20 minutes and remove the towel.

Turn on the oven to 400° F. Bake 45 to 50 minutes, or until the loaves are browned and sound hollow when rapped on the bottom. Makes 3 loaves.

---

Q. *I am getting tired of making sourdough bread. Can I give my starter a rest for a while?*

A. You don't have to bake bread, but you do have to feed the starter. Just take out the amount you usually use and replace it with a simple water-and-flour dough of the same consistency.

# Hazelnut Bread

*David Liederman, the creator of David's Cookies, ran a restaurant that served excellent Sunday brunches. In the bread basket were slices of toast made from this bread. I coaxed the recipe from Liederman.*

In a small cup or bowl, combine the yeast and milk. Let it stand about 5 minutes until it begins to foam, indicating that the yeast is coming to life.

Meanwhile, in a mixing bowl, beat the sugar and eggs until the sugar is dissolved. Beat in the softened butter, flour, and salt. Now add the yeast mixture. Mix it in thoroughly and knead or beat in the nuts. The dough will be fairly sticky, but just turn it out into a medium-size loaf pan and let it rise in a warm place until it doubles in bulk. This can take 2 hours.

Bake the loaf at 425° F. for 30 minutes, or until the bread is nicely browned and a knife or skewer inserted into the middle comes out dry. Let the loaf cool, then slice it up and serve it with breakfast or as a snack.

1½ packages active dry yeast
¼ cup milk, warmed to 105 to 115° F.
2 tablespoons sugar
3 large eggs
4 tablespoons (½ stick) butter at room temperature
2 cups sifted flour
½ teaspoon salt
1 cup coarsely chopped or ground hazelnuts (filberts)

# Risotto with Red Wine

*At an Easter meal in Tuscany, the wife of a prominent winemaker made this seemingly extravagant, but really very simple, dish. It has an unforgettable flavor. For this and the following risotto recipes, use Italian arborio rice, a short-grain rice that has the unique property of contributing its starch to the cooking liquid without losing its firm texture.*

1 medium onion
2 cloves garlic
¼ cup extra-virgin olive oil
1 branch rosemary
2 or 3 fresh sage leaves
1 bay leaf
1½ cups *arborio* rice
1 bottle good red wine
2 tablespoons butter
⅓ cup grated Parmesan

Chop the onion and garlic. In a 3-quart saucepan, heat the olive oil and sauté the onion and garlic with the herbs until the onion is soft, 3 to 4 minutes. Add the rice and stir well to coat. Add the wine and cook 15 minutes, or until the wine is absorbed and the rice is almost done.

Have 1 cup of boiling stock or water ready. Add half of the water to finish cooking the rice; use the remaining ½ cup only if necessary. Cook until the texture of the rice is firm but not crunchy, and the mixture is soupy but thick. Remove the herbs and stir in the butter and grated Parmesan. Makes 4 servings.

# Winter Squash Risotto

*Winter squash makes a beautiful pale golden risotto, and the soft, ripe teleme cheese makes the dish meltingly smooth and creamy.*

Melt the butter in a skillet over medium heat. Add the rice and squash, and cook gently, stirring occasionally, for about 10 minutes without browning. Turn the heat to low and begin adding the broth, ½ cup at a time, waiting until each previous addition is absorbed before pouring in another—total cooking time is about 20 to 25 minutes. Stir occasionally during this time. The rice will slowly become creamy and tender. Add the teleme cheese and stir constantly until it melts. Season with salt and pepper, stir in the parsley and serve. Makes 3 or 4 servings.

*Microwave directions:* In a 2- or 3-quart microwavable dish, melt the butter for 30 seconds on high. Stir in the rice and squash to coat with the butter. Microwave for 2 minutes on full power. Add the broth. Microwave for 5 minutes on full power, and then for 12 minutes at half power. Stir in the cheese, salt and pepper to taste, and parsley.

3 tablespoons butter
1 cup *arborio* rice
2 cups thinly sliced winter squash, such as butternut or acorn (peel and seed squash before measuring)
3½ cups chicken broth
4 ounces teleme cheese, diced
Salt and freshly ground pepper
2 tablespoons chopped parsley

---

Q. *Do sulfites affect the aging of wine?*

A. Because it has a preservative effect, sulfur dioxide tends to keep wine fresher as it ages, a positive benefit. Also, as wine ages, the sulfur dioxide tends to bind with oxygen in the wine into a form that has no known effect on humans. Therefore, aged wines have less sulfur dioxide in them than young wines do. Young sweet wines tend to have the highest levels.

# Risotto al Limone

*From Lorenza de' Medici, whose cooking school in Chianti, Italy, is a favorite with visiting Americans.*

1 small onion
4 tablespoons (½ stick) unsalted butter
½ cup marrow or 2 tablespoons extra-virgin olive oil
2 cups *arborio* rice
6 cups meat broth, heated
1 cup grated Parmesan
¼ cup chopped parsley
Grated zest and juice of 1 lemon
Salt and freshly ground pepper

Chop onion fine and cook with half of the butter and all the marrow on moderate heat, stirring constantly.

Add rice; after a couple of minutes, start adding the boiling broth, stirring always, ½ cup at a time, after the previously added is absorbed. The rice should always be covered by a veil of broth. Keep the broth itself at a low boil.

When rice is cooked, after approximately 15 minutes, add the Parmesan, the rest of the butter, parsley, lemon zest and juice, and salt and pepper to taste. Cover and let it rest for a couple of minutes before serving. The risotto should be creamy, with a porridge-like consistency. Makes 6 first-course servings.

*Microwave directions:* Combine the chopped onion and butter in a 3-quart microwave bowl. Cover and microwave on full power for 5 minutes. Add the rice and 5½ cups broth. Cover and microwave on full power for 5 minutes, and then on half power for 12 minutes. The rice should be just about done. If not, cook on half power 1 minute longer. Stir in remaining ingredients.

# Risotto con Grappa

*Unlike wine-flavored risotto, if you use too much grappa, this risotto will taste harsh. Save just a splash to stir in at the end. When I had this dish at Castello di Querceto, a Chianti wine estate, I could not place the spicy flavor of the grappa until the cook told me what she had used.*

Finely chop the onion and garlic. In a medium to large saucepan, sauté the onion and garlic in the olive oil until they are soft, about 5 minutes. Stir in the rice to coat with the oil, then add ¼ cup of the grappa and a ladle of broth. Stir the mixture until it is absorbed, then add more broth. Keep adding and stirring for about 15 minutes, or until the rice is just barely cooked through. Add the remaining grappa, butter, Parmesan, and salt and pepper to taste. The mixture should be slightly soupy. Add a few more tablespoons of broth if necessary. Makes 4 servings.

1 onion
1 clove garlic
3 tablespoons olive oil
1 cup *arborio* rice
⅓ cup grappa
About 3 cups chicken broth, simmering
2 tablespoons butter
¼ cup grated Parmesan
Salt and freshly ground pepper

Q. *Is there a way to make risotto partially in advance and then finish it at the last minute?*

A. I have Judy Rogers, the chef at San Francisco's highly regarded Zuni Café, to thank for this method. She uses it whenever they have a special risotto on the menu to serve à la carte. Prepare the risotto by the standard method but stop before making the last addition of broth. Turn the partially cooked risotto out onto a baking sheet. Spread it out so that it cools quickly. Do not refrigerate.

To finish the risotto, put the right number of servings and the final addition of broth into a saucepan to heat through. Adjust the texture with broth, butter and grated Parmesan cheese.

# Salsa Spaghetti

*A jar of salsa or picante sauce sort of looks like marinara, but it tastes different and fresher, for a wonderful change of pace.*

½ pound spaghetti or spaghettini
3 tablespoons olive oil
1 jar (8 ounces) salsa or picante sauce, hot, medium, or mild
1½ cups (6 ounces) grated jack cheese

Cook the spaghetti in plenty of boiling, salted water until done. Drain well, and place in a large warmed bowl. Toss briefly with the olive oil, then add the salsa and cheese, and toss several more times, until blended and the cheese melts slightly. Serve immediately. Makes 2 or 3 servings.

---

Q. *Is there a way to make risotto in the microwave oven?*

A. You bet. I do it all the time. It saves having to stand by the stove. Although the texture isn't quite the same, it is much less bothersome.

For 4 servings, I use **1 cup arborio rice** and **2¾ cups broth**. Chop **1 small onion** and **2 cloves garlic**. Place them in a microwavable bowl with **2 to 3 tablespoons olive oil**. Cover the bowl and microwave on high for 5 minutes. Add the rice and broth, but save ¼ cup of the broth. Add a **pinch of saffron (optional)** and **1 bay leaf**. Cover and microwave on high 5 minutes to bring the broth to a boil, then microwave on 50 percent power for 12 minutes.

Stir in the reserved broth, **¼ cup freshly grated Parmesan**, and **1 or 2 pats of butter**. Remove and discard the bay leaf. Season to taste with **salt and freshly ground pepper**. Done.

# Hot and Spicy Noodles

*From my friend Maggie Gin, known for her line of bottled Chinese sauces, comes this home-style method of serving the noodles and meat sauce separately. This makes it easier than most Chinese noodle recipes. If Chinese egg noodles are not available, use any fresh pasta.*

Bring a large pot of water to a boil. Salt it lightly. Boil the noodles in the water. Drain them well and toss with a bit of corn oil or Oriental sesame oil. The noodles may be served at room temperature, if you prefer to prepare them in advance.

In a wok or skillet, heat the corn oil and stir-fry the meat until it loses its redness, about 2 minutes. Add the remaining ingredients, except the onions, and stir-fry for 2 minutes. Transfer to a warm serving bowl and sprinkle with green onions. Serve this sauce on the side, with noodles. Makes 4 main-course servings.

1 pound fresh Chinese egg noodles
½ cup corn oil
1 pound ground lean pork, beef, or lamb
1 clove garlic, minced
2 teaspoons grated fresh ginger
Pinch hot-pepper flakes
3 tablespoons soy sauce
½ cup chopped green onions (garnish)

# Spaghetti with Green Tomatoes

*This is a wonderful use for tomatoes that haven't quite gotten red enough. The best ones are right off the vine, but even if they're supermarket tomatoes, the refreshing acidity of the greenish tomatoes makes a nice balance to the olive oil. This dish was inspired by a restaurant in Milan called Da Armando.*

1 pound tomatoes, slightly green
1 pound spaghetti
3 cloves garlic
3 tablespoons extra-virgin olive oil
Salt and freshly ground pepper
¼ cup grated Parmesan, or more to
   taste

Bring 1 gallon (4 quarts) water to a boil. Drop the tomatoes into the water for 15 seconds. Remove and let cool. Keep the water boiling. Add the spaghetti and 2 tablespoons salt.

While the spaghetti is boiling, peel the tomatoes and squeeze out the seeds. Chop the tomatoes coarsely. Chop the garlic fine. In a skillet, sauté the garlic in olive oil gently for 2 minutes. Add the chopped tomato and turn up the heat. Cook 3 to 4 minutes, until the tomatoes soften. Add salt and pepper to taste. Drain the spaghetti, and toss with the sauce and the grated Parmesan. Makes 4 servings.

# Spaghetti with Broccoli

*Lorenza de' Medici of Badia a Coltibuono in Chianti, Italy, shared this recipe of hers with the "KCBS Kitchen" audience.*

**C**ut the florets off the broccoli and set them aside. Peel the broccoli stems, and cut them into ½- to ¾-inch chunks.

In a medium skillet over moderate heat, place ¼ cup of the olive oil. Sauté the bread crumbs with the garlic, anchovy, and pepper until the crumbs are golden brown and crisp. Set them aside.

Bring a large pot of water to a boil. Add 1 tablespoon salt for each half gallon of water. Add the broccoli stems and boil for 5 minutes. Add the spaghetti and the florets. Boil for 6 minutes, or until the spaghetti is cooked al dente. Drain well and toss with the remaining olive oil and the bread crumb mixture. Makes 4 to 6 servings.

1 bunch broccoli
½ cup olive oil
1 clove garlic, finely chopped
2 anchovy fillets, mashed
1 cup dry bread crumbs
1 small dry chili pepper (optional)
1 pound spaghetti

---

**Q.** *How do Chinese restaurants get their broccoli so bright green? Mine always comes out sort of khaki when I steam it.*

**A.** Vegetables keep their color when they are cooked in plenty of boiling water in open pots. Nutrition zealots claim that steamed vegetables are better, but it's just not so. Ever look at the water at the bottom of the steamer? That's where much of the nutrition goes, and the color. There are natural acids in green vegetables that dilute the color if they are trapped in the same container as the vegetables, as happens in steaming.

As far as I am concerned, there are two good ways to cook green vegetables: boiling in plenty of salty water and microwaving.

# Rigatoni Ratatouille

*To cut down on the usually heavy dose of olive oil used to make ratatouille, the vegetables here are just brushed with oil and baked, instead of stewed in oil. With all the basil and parsley, this is a classic refreshing summer dish.*

1 eggplant (about 1 pound)
2 zucchini (about ½ pound)
Salt
Olive oil
12 ounces rigatoni
4 tomatoes (about 1 pound)
1 cup or more fresh basil leaves, cut
  or torn into small pieces
½ cup chopped parsley
Grated Parmesan

Cut the eggplant and zucchini into strips about 2 inches long, 1 inch wide, and ½ inch thick. It is not necessary to be precise. Sprinkle lightly with salt on both sides, then arrange in a single layer on a baking sheet covered with paper towels. Cover with more paper towels and another baking sheet, and weight down with a brick or heavy can. Let sit for about 3 hours—or overnight if more convenient. Wash the vegetables under running water and pat them dry. Arrange on a baking sheet or jelly roll pan, brush lightly with olive oil, cover with foil, and bake in a preheated 350° F. oven for 20 minutes, until soft but not mushy. This may be completed in advance.

Before serving, drop the pasta into a large pot of boiling salted water. Meanwhile, peel, seed and chop the tomatoes. Film the bottom of a large skillet or Dutch oven with olive oil and place over medium heat. Add the tomatoes and cook gently for several minutes. When the pasta is done, drain well and add to the tomatoes along with the cooked eggplant and zucchini. Stir together gently for several minutes, until heated through. Stir in the basil and turn the mixture onto a large platter. Sprinkle with parsley and take to the table. Pass the cheese separately. Makes 4 to 6 servings.

# Orzo with Scallops

*Tiny orzo is the pasta that seems to work best in this dish. The peas and scallops don't slide off the rice-shaped grains. Be sure the skillet is hot, however—the oil should be almost smoking—or the scallops will sweat rather than brown (which isn't a disaster; they just don't look as nice).*

The scallop mixture doesn't take more than about 2 minutes to prepare, so have all ingredients at hand when you start. Begin by boiling the orzo in lots of salted water.

Heat the oil in a large skillet. (Cast iron is best, or use heavy aluminum.) When it is just beginning to smoke, it's hot enough. Immediately drop in the scallops, then stir and toss rapidly for about 1 minute. Add the peas and toss about 30 seconds more, to heat through. Pour in the cream and season to taste with salt and pepper, then toss with the chives or parsley. Drain the pasta well and scoop it onto a large platter or shallow serving dish. Pour the scallop and pea mixture over the top and serve immediately. Makes 3 or 4 servings.

½ pound orzo (rice-shaped pasta)
3 tablespoons olive oil
½ pound tiny bay scallops or large scallops, cut into small pieces
2 cups cooked green peas or frozen peas, thawed
¼ cup whipping cream
Salt and freshly ground pepper
2 tablespoons chopped fresh chives or parsley

Q. *How can I prepare eggplant without using so much oil?*

A. Eggplant absorbs oil like a sponge. Here is a method for making browned eggplant slices that uses much less oil than frying:

Cut the eggplant into ½-inch slices. Place the slices on an oiled baking sheet. Brush lightly with more oil. Use extra-virgin olive oil or walnut oil for best flavor. Bake in a 475° F. oven for 5 minutes, or until the eggplant starts to turn brown. Turn the slices with a spatula and bake 5 to 10 minutes longer, or until the eggplant is cooked through and browned.

# Cottage and Cream Cheese Gnocchi

*These are easier to make than the traditional potato gnocchi (Italian style dumplings), because you can mix these in a food processor. Potatoes would turn to glue. These can be poached hours in advance, then browned in the oven with a dusting of cheese and butter just before serving with a green salad, or as a side dish to roast meat or poultry.*

2 cups (1 pint carton) cottage cheese
½ pound (8-ounce bar) cream cheese
    at room temperature
2 eggs
1 cup flour
1 cup finely grated Parmesan
Salt and freshly ground pepper
4 to 6 tablespoons (½ to ¾ stick)
    melted butter

Whirl the cottage cheese in the food processor until smooth, or force through a very fine mesh strainer or sieve. Add the cream cheese and beat until blended. Add the eggs, flour, ½ cup of the Parmesan, and salt and pepper to taste; mix until thoroughly combined.

Have a large pot of simmering water on the stove, and butter a large baking dish, such as a 9 × 13-inch oval.

Drop heaping teaspoons of the cheese mixture into the barely simmering water, nudging them off the spoon with your wet fingertip. Do only one-third to one-half of the mixture at a time. Poach for about 3 minutes, then remove with a slotted spoon to the buttered baking dish. Simmer the remaining gnocchi the same way, transferring them to the dish as they are done. Drizzle with the melted butter and sprinkle with the remaining ½ cup grated Parmesan. Cover and refrigerate if not baked within a couple hours.

Bake in a preheated 375° F. oven for 20 to 30 minutes, until the gnocchi have puffed slightly and they are lightly browned and bubbling. Serve immediately. Makes 4 to 6 servings.

# Ravioli Piedmont Style

*Giorgio Rocca, owner of Giardino da Felicin in Italy's Piedmont region, showed me how to form these three-sided ravioli. In place of white cheese, use Mexican* queso blanco *or allow 1 pound of ricotta to drip through a sieve for several hours. Do not use a stringy cheese such as Monterey Jack.*

First make the pasta. Put the ingredients in a food processor and let it run until it forms a crumbly mixture. Knead and roll it out in a pasta machine to a thickness of about 1/16 inch (about number 6 on the setting). Keep the pasta covered so it does not dry.

Mix the ingredients for the filling, and chop them fine together in a food processor, or grind them well. The texture should be fine and moist, but not pasty.

To form the ravioli, place a sheet of pasta on the edge of a cutting board, long side facing you. Take some of the filling on a large spoon. With a butter knife, transfer 1/2-teaspoon blobs onto the pasta, 1 inch apart. It's okay if the blobs touch the edge. Fold the edge of the pasta over the blobs to form a long tube that covers them completely. Press the edge of the pasta to the bottom sheet to make a seam that encloses the filling. Roll the cutter over this seam to seal it and cut it. You should now have a long tube with lumps of filling visible.

Pinch this tube between the blobs. Don't press down, pinch. Roll the cutter through the pinched places to cut the tube into individual ravioli. Place the finished ravioli in single layers on a floured tray. Cover with plastic wrap and refrigerate.

Boil the ravioli in salted water for 2 to 3 minutes. Serve them with leftover roast beef juice, or butter melted with fresh sage or basil leaves, or with a meat-tomato sauce on the side. Makes 6 servings.

**Pasta:**
3 large eggs
2 1/4 cups flour, more or less
3/4 teaspoon salt

**Filling:**
1 cup (4 ounces) crumbled white cheese
6 to 8 ounces (about 1 cup) well-seasoned roast beef
3 or 4 green onions or 2 zucchini, diced and sautéed
3 or 4 leaves fresh sage or your choice of fresh herb
1 or 2 slices stale bread, soaked in milk and squeezed dry

# Red Pepper Pasta

*If you have a food processor and either an electric or hand-cranked pasta machine, making your own pasta takes little more time than making a meat loaf. The only chore here is roasting and peeling the pepper, but that can be done a day or two ahead. The results are lovely pale orange strands of pasta with a mild pepper flavor.*

1 red bell pepper, roasted, peeled, and seeded (page 151)
1½ cups flour
½ teaspoon salt
¼ cup beaten egg (about 1½ eggs)

Puree the pepper in a food processor fitted with the metal blade. Add the flour, salt, and egg, and let the machine run until the dough forms a ball that spins around the bowl—about 15 to 30 seconds. If the dough remains dry and crumbly, add a few drops of water or another teaspoon or so of egg and process again. Once mixed, let the dough spin around the bowl for about 20 seconds—this is the "kneading." Wrap the dough in plastic wrap and refrigerate for at least an hour (or overnight) before continuing.

Roll out the chilled dough according to the instructions for your wringer-type pasta machine, either electric or hand cranked, and cut it into narrow noodles, like fettuccine. The cut noodles may be boiled immediately, or draped over a broom handle to dry out a bit. Makes enough to serve 4 as a first course or 2 to 3 as a main course.

Q. *I have heard that the best pasta is made with durum wheat. Should I use it in my homemade noodles?*

A. Durum is a high-protein wheat that makes pasta firm, perfect for dried shapes. I prefer all-purpose flour for homemade pasta that is going to be served fresh, especially for ravioli or tortellini. The texture is better.

# Garlic Parmesan Noodles

*Putting all the flavors into the noodles instead of onto the noodles is a good way to simplify final preparation. Just add a little butter or olive oil.*

Combine the flour, salt, and garlic in the food processor. Blend for about 30 seconds, until the flour is filled with the aroma and taste of garlic. Add the oil, Parmesan, and eggs and process a few seconds. Drop in the parsley leaves and continue processing until the dough forms a ball, about 15 seconds or so. If it's too sticky, add a couple of tablespoons of flour. If it's too dry to form a ball, add a few drops of water.

Turn the dough onto a surface and knead it by hand for another 3 minutes, until very smooth. Wrap it in plastic wrap, and let dough rest for at least 30 minutes (or overnight in the refrigerator). Form noodles and cook as in previous recipe. Top or toss with your favorite pasta sauce, or just butter the noodles lightly. Makes 2 or 3 servings.

1 ½ cups flour
½ teaspoons salt
2 large cloves garlic
1 tablespoon olive oil
½ cup (about 3 ounces) finely grated Parmesan
2 eggs
About 24 leaves Italian parsley

Q. *What type of pasta maker do you recommend?*

A. In the past few years we have seen a lot of electric pasta machines that work on what I call the sausage principle. You put the ingredients into the machine, which mixes them up to make a dough, and then extrudes the pasta through a disk that determines the shape. I have never found this pasta to be as good as the type made the old-fashioned way.

Fortunately, there are machines that can mix the dough. They are called food processors, which most of us already have. There are also machines to form and cut the dough, cranked by hand or machine. They are also easier to clean up than the extruder-type pasta makers. I recommend these relatively inexpensive hand-crank machines.

# Spinach Rice Loaf

*Months after giving this recipe on the air, I was still getting requests for it. When you serve it cold, it makes a great accompaniment to sandwiches. Or serve it as an appetizer.*

1 large onion
3 tablespoons olive oil
4 large cloves garlic
2 large bunches spinach (about 2
    pounds), washed and chopped
1 cup uncooked long-grain white rice
1½ cups tomato sauce
1½ cups water
½ teaspoon salt
½ teaspoon freshly ground pepper

Chop the onion and mince the garlic. Heat the oil in a large saucepan, add the onion and cook gently for 5 minutes. Add the garlic and cook 1 minute more. Add the spinach and cook, stirring, until the spinach is limp and wilted—about 3 minutes. Add the rice, tomato sauce, water, salt, and pepper, bring to a boil, stir well, then cover and simmer gently for about 45 minutes, stirring 2 or 3 times.

Serve hot or turn the mixture into a large oiled loaf pan and chill for several hours, until firm. Turn out of the pan, slice, and serve with tomato vinaigrette and crumbled feta. Makes 6 servings.

Q. *I can never get brown rice to come out right. It is either too dry or too soupy. What is the trick?*

A. The nutrition zealots hate it when I suggest this, but it is by far the best way to ensure perfectly cooked brown rice. Boil it like pasta, in plenty of water, for 25 to 35 minutes. When it is done to the right texture—try a bite to be sure—drain it well and toss it with whatever seasonings you like. Never fails.

# Baked Polenta and Prawns

*The prawns cook in the midst of a tasty fish-flavored polenta. It comes out like a great casserole.*

Shell, devein, and cut the prawns in ½-inch bits. Set aside.

Bring the water, stock, salt, and pepper to a boil in a large, heavy pan. Slowly add the cornmeal in a thin stream, whisking or stirring constantly. Continue to cook, stirring frequently, for 15 to 20 minutes, until the mixture is quite thick and holds its shape. (Wear long sleeves and keep the pan covered with a round fine mesh screen—a spatter shield—so the polenta doesn't sputter all over you.)

Preheat the oven to 350° F.

Remove from heat and stir in the prawns, tomatoes, 2 tablespoons of the butter, and ½ cup of the Parmesan. Drop the mixture by tablespoons over the bottom of a buttered 9 × 13-inch baking dish—it looks more interesting than if simply dumped in and smoothed with a spatula; the top should be rough and pebbly. Dot with the remaining butter, sprinkle with the remaining Parmesan, scatter several sage leaves over the top, and bake for 20 minutes, until bubbly and light brown. Makes 4 to 6 servings.

¾ pound (about 12) jumbo prawns
2 cups water
2 cups fish stock or 1 cup clam juice thinned with 1 cup water
1½ teaspoons salt
½ teaspoon freshly ground pepper
1 cup cornmeal
1 cup peeled, seeded, and chopped tomatoes, fresh or canned
6 tablespoons (¾ stick) butter
¾ cup grated Parmesan
Sage leaves

# Barley "Pilaf"

*Cook any whole grain as you would a rice pilaf and it makes a delicious dish. Add a bit of meat to make a one-dish meal. Lamb is especially good.*

4 tablespoons (½ stick) butter
1 onion, chopped
1 cup pearl barley
5 cups chicken or beef stock, heated
1 to 2 cups diced cooked meat
   (optional)
½ cup freshly grated Parmesan, plus
   some to pass at the table

Melt the butter in a large skillet. Add the onion and cook gently for about 5 minutes. Add the barley and cook gently 3 or 4 more minutes, stirring frequently. Add ½ cup of broth and stir well.

Continue to add ½ cup of broth every 5 minutes or so, stirring frequently, and waiting until each previous addition is almost absorbed by the barley before adding more broth. Total cooking time will be about 50 minutes—although you can carry on with other things in the kitchen simultaneously. Add the meat and stir until heated through. Just before serving, stir in the Parmesan.

If you are making this ahead, omit the cheese. Then, when you reheat it, add a little water or stock if the mixture is too thick, and stir in the Parmesan before serving. Pass more cheese at the table.

Unlike risotto, this dish reheats well. Omit the meat, if you wish, and simply serve it as a side dish. Makes 4 servings as a main course with meat, 6 to 8 servings as a side dish without meat.

# Scotch Oatmeal

*John Tovey, owner and chef of Miller Howe Inn, Lake Windermere, England, is famous for his bracing oatmeal that is creamy and rich. The secret is long cooking in a mixture of milk and water and a final enhancement of single malt Scotch whisky. That would warm you up on a chill North Country morning.*

Soak the oats in the milk overnight in the top of a double boiler. About 30 to 45 minutes before serving, have water boiling in the bottom half of the double boiler, then stir the 2 cups of boiling water called for in the recipe into the oats and milk along with the salt. Let them cook gently in the top of the double boiler for 25 to 30 minutes or until the cereal is creamy. Stir in the brown sugar and 1 tablespoon of butter and turn off the heat under the double boiler.

Alternately, you can cook the oatmeal in a saucepan over low heat, but keep stirring it to keep it from sticking.

Serve the oatmeal with a 1-teaspoon pat of butter to melt on top of it and a drizzle of Scotch whisky, if desired. Makes 4 real servings (that is, large and hearty).

2 cups old-fashioned oatmeal or
  rolled oats
2 cups milk
2 cups boiling water
¾ teaspoon salt
3 to 4 tablespoons brown sugar
1 tablespoon butter
4 teaspoons butter, in 4 pats
8 teaspoons Scotch whisky, preferably
  single malt (optional)

# CHAPTER FOUR:

# "SIDES"

# "SIDES"

These are the foods that make a meal complete. Some of my favorite recipes in this book reside in this catchall chapter, a collection of side dishes, middle-of-the-meal courses, drinks, and other dishes that landed here because they don't fit into any of the other chapters. In some cases they don't even fit neatly into a meal. Instead they are snacks.

Because today's eating habits emphasize vegetables and salads, a healthy percentage of the recipes offered on the "KCBS Kitchen" fall into these categories. There are more salad dressing recipes in this book than cookie recipes, a ratio that reflects the lineup of recipes on the program. Although I seldom make a special salad dressing when I am cooking for myself (an Italian-style coating of olive oil sprinkled with lemon juice or vinegar, salt, and pepper dresses any respectable collection of fresh greens), I like to vary the dressing ingredients when cooking for guests. Over the years, I have wheedled some of the most delicious house dressing recipes from restaurants around the country. Two favorites of longtime listeners are the creamy C. K.'s Salad Dressing (page 175) and the onion-miso-based Spiral Salad Dressing (page 179), both coincidentally from Florida restaurants.

I have the same attitude toward vegetables. Most of the time, I just boil them in plenty of salted water until they are barely cooked through—firm but no longer crunchy—and toss them with a bit of butter or olive oil. Lately, I have been using the microwave oven more and more for green vegetables and squashes. It is worth the time spent getting the feel for how to time them, because the results are more flavorful than boiling or steaming. When I am cooking vegetables for a dinner party, I always select something that does not have to be timed carefully at the last minute. Boiling or microwaving vegetables until they are barely done, then cooling them rapidly in running cold water, readies them for quick reheating at the last minute in a large sauté pan with olive oil or butter. Stir or toss them quickly over a moderate to high flame until they reheat, about 1 minute.

You will find that in this chapter, especially, but throughout the book, I give quantities of vegetables by weight (1 pound tomatoes) or by number (1 small onion) rather than by volume (½ cup diced onion). There are two reasons. The first is that this is how you buy vegetables. You don't buy a half cup of onion, you buy one. You don't buy 2 cups of tomatoes, you buy a pound. The second reason is that, once you cut up an onion and measure ½ cup, what do you do with the remaining few tablespoons? Save it in a plastic bag? Waste it? I say use it. Most vegetable recipes are not so sensitive that they will be ruined by using a somewhat larger or smaller amount of the ingredient. Besides, clinical accuracy in the kitchen is not necessary except when preparing pastries and custards.

# THE SECRET TO GOOD COFFEE

I developed this technique after interviewing an inventor who once developed products for a large manufacturer of coffee makers. He discovered that all the good flavors were extracted from ground coffee in 2 minutes 45 seconds. After that, most of what you got was weak and bitter. If you've ever watched a drip coffee maker at work, you may have noticed that the last bit of water has very little color. The truth is, it has little flavor, too.

He invented a coffee maker that carefully measured just the right amount of hot water to go through the coffee grounds in 2 minutes 45 seconds. That wasn't enough water to make a full pot of coffee, so he designed a device that sent the rest of the water around the coffee.

Some 30 prototypes of this machine were made, but the company never manufactured or marketed them. I tasted coffee made with one of these machines, and it was the best I've ever had.

I like to make coffee with a drip cone and filter. It's cheaper than a machine, and I don't mind pouring the hot water from the tea-kettle through the cone. Applying the inventor's 2-minute 45-second principle to my plain filter cone, I discovered that it took just about that long for two cones full of water to pass through. That's how this technique was born:

1. Use a drip cone and paper filter. Use 1 measure of ground coffee for each cup of coffee you want to make.
2. Boil enough water to make the right amount of coffee.
3. Pour the hot water over the coffee grounds to fill the cone. When it has dripped through, fill the cone with hot water a second time. Let it drip through.
4. Remove the cone and add enough hot water to the pot to fill it to the right level. (Most coffee pots are marked with cup measurements.)

Don't worry about adding what may seem like a lot of water to the pot. It won't be weak. Most of the flavor was extracted in the first pour. It should be the best coffee you've ever made.

# Anytime Lemonade

*So much lemonade these days starts off powdered in a package that you may have forgotten how good the fresh stuff can be. The lemonade mix below can be prepared and kept in the refrigerator ready to make a fresh glass anytime, hence the name.*

For 2 glasses:
1 juicy lemon
6 tablespoons sugar
6 tablespoons water

Squeeze the lemon and strain the juice into two 12-ounce glasses. Add some ice, to your taste. (I like to fill the glass at least ¾ full.) Put the sugar and at least as much water into a saucepan along with the lemon zest and turn on the heat. As soon as the sugar has dissolved, turn off the heat and divide the syrup between the glasses. Add water to fill. Some of the ice will melt, but the drink will be cold. Add more ice if you like.

# Lemonade Syrup

*Follow these guidelines for making up quantities in advance.*

6 lemons
2 cups sugar
1 cup water

Squeeze the lemons. Strain the juice and set it aside. Cut two of the lemons into small strips and put them in a saucepan with the sugar and water. Heat the mixture until the sugar dissolves. Combine the syrup and the lemon juice in a jar and keep it refrigerated. This stays fairly fresh for a day or two.

To make a glass of lemonade, stir 2 tablespoons of the lemon syrup into a glass of ice water.

# Berry Buttermilk Refresher

*This makes a terrific mid-afternoon snack. Prepare the berries and keep them refrigerated for at least an hour or so to dissolve the sugar thoroughly. If you use artificial sweetener, this step is not necessary. Use raspberries, boysenberries, marionberries, olallieberries, blackberries, or strawberries.*

Lightly crush the berries and mix them with the sugar and vanilla. Cover the bowl and put the mixture in the refrigerator for at least 1 hour. This will keep two or three days.

Place in blender and puree. (*Note:* you may want to strain out raspberry seeds.)

**For each cup of fresh berries:**
¼ cup sugar or equivalent in artificial sweetener
½ teaspoon vanilla extract

**For each serving:**
¼ cup sweetened berry mixture
¼ cup crushed ice (optional)
1 cup thick buttermilk (Bulgarian culture is excellent)

LOW CALORIE · LOW FAT

# Party Eggnog

*A rich, old-fashioned version in sufficient quantity for most holiday parties. For smaller groups, you can cut the recipe in half or by quarters.*

12 eggs, separated
1 cup sugar
1 quart milk
2 cups bourbon
1 cup sherry or Madeira
4 cups whipping cream, whipped
Nutmeg

In a large bowl, beat the egg yolks with the sugar until smooth. Add the milk, bourbon, and sherry. Beat the egg whites until they stand in soft peaks. Fold them into the yolk mixture. Whip the cream lightly and fold it into the mixture, gently but thoroughly. Serve it cold with freshly grated nutmeg on top. Makes 25 to 30 servings.

# Alcohol-free Quick Eggnog

*It is always a good idea to make a batch of nonalcoholic nog for those who want to take it easy. This is also slightly less caloric.*

6 eggs, separated
3 tablespoons sugar
Dash salt
1 cup milk
½ cup cream
1 teaspoon vanilla extract
Dash nutmeg

Beat the egg yolks with the sugar, salt, milk, cream, and vanilla until smooth. Beat the egg whites in a separate bowl to soft peaks and fold them into the mixture. Top with nutmeg. Makes about 5 to 6 cups.

# Turkey Gravy

*The secret to good gravy is to do everything possible to get as much flavor and as smooth a texture as possible. For the flavor, make stock from the bones and start with chicken stock to make it even richer. For the texture, remember that the gravy will thicken as it cools, so make it thinner in the saucepan than you want it to be on the plate.*

Put the neck, giblets, and trimmings in a small saucepan. Break the celery and carrot in half. Cut the onion in half and stick a clove in each half. Add the vegetables along with the bay leaf and parsley to the saucepan, and cover them with 2 ½ cups of water or chicken stock. Bring the mixture to a boil, lower the heat to simmer, cover the pan, and let it cook for 2 hours. Strain the stock. You should have 2 cups.

Chop the giblets if you like to add them to the sauce.

In a clean saucepan, melt the butter or turkey fat and stir in the flour. Cook, stirring constantly, until the raw flour aroma dissipates. Add the stock and cook the sauce until it thickens and begins to simmer. Let it simmer for 10 minutes. You can do this in advance and reheat the sauce. If you keep the sauce for longer than a few minutes, rub the surface with butter to make a thin coating to prevent a crust from forming.

When the turkey is done, pour all the juices into a tall, narrow cup or into a fat separator. Let the fat rise to the top, and pour the brown juice underneath into the saucepan with the sauce. Put the roasting pan over heat, and deglaze any browned bits with ½ cup water. Let it boil, scraping up the browned bits to dissolve them. Add them to the saucepan; season the gravy to taste with salt and pepper.

If the gravy is too thick, add some stock or milk. If it is too thin, dissolve 1 tablespoon cornstarch in 1 tablespoon water. Stir this into the simmering stock 1 teaspoon at a time, allowing 30 seconds for it to thicken before adding more if necessary. Gravy should be about the consistency of heavy cream. Don't make it too thick. It will thicken as it cools in the sauceboat.

**Turkey stock:**
**Neck, heart, and gizzard, plus any trimmings from the turkey**
**1 rib celery**
**1 carrot**
**1 small onion**
**2 cloves**
**1 bay leaf**
**2 or 3 large sprigs parsley (stems are okay)**
**2 ½ cups water or chicken stock**

**Gravy:**
**3 tablespoons butter or turkey fat**
**3 tablespoons flour**

# Mushroom-Clam Sauce

*I have always enjoyed sauces made with fish broth. Lacking fish broth, you can use bottled clam juice, as in this easy-to-assemble sauce.*

3 ounces mushrooms, thinly sliced
1 shallot or ½ medium onion, finely chopped
1 clove garlic, finely chopped
2 tablespoons oil
½ teaspoon dried basil
1 carrot, thinly sliced
1 cup (8 ounces) bottled clam juice
Salt and freshly ground pepper
1 tablespoon arrowroot
2 tablespoons butter

In a medium-size saucepan over moderate heat, sauté the mushrooms with the shallot and garlic in the oil. After 2 or 3 minutes, when the vegetables are soft, add the basil, carrot, and clam juice. Bring to a boil and reduce heat to a simmer. Season to taste with salt and pepper.

Dissolve the arrowroot in 1 tablespoon water. Stir it into the simmering sauce. Remove it from the heat and stir in the butter. Serve over grilled fish, chicken, or pasta. Makes 1¾ cups, enough for 6 servings.

# Elaine Bell's Red Pepper Sauce

*A successful and creative caterer in Sonoma and culinary director of Sterling Vineyards in Napa Valley, Elaine Bell created this sauce to serve with a pasta salad at a Sonoma County Wine Auction. I persuaded her to share the recipe.*

Char the peppers under a broiler or over a flame, turning them often. The skin must be blistered all over. Let the peppers cool in a plastic bag or wrapped in a towel, then remove the skin. Cut them open and remove the seeds and pith. Puree the peppers in a food processor.

Add the green onions, eggs, lemon juice, salt, and pepper. Process the mixture for a few seconds, then start adding the oil with the machine running. It should emulsify like mayonnaise.

Check seasoning. Serve with grilled poultry, fish, or meat. It is also terrific on pasta or vegetables. Makes about 2 ½ cups.

**2 red bell peppers
2 tablespoons chopped green onions
1 egg at room temperature
1 ½ teaspoons lemon juice
¼ teaspoon salt
⅛ teaspoon white pepper
1 ½ cups salad oil**

---

**Q.** *Do you know an easy way to peel and roast sweet red bell peppers?*

**A.** This is the method taught to me by the late Joe Carcione. It results in very sweet roasted peppers that lack only the smoky taste of the charring method. Arrange the peppers in a baking pan and place them in a 350° F. oven for 1 hour, or until they start to deflate. Turn off the oven and cover the peppers with a clean towel. Leave them in the oven to cool gradually for at least two hours, or overnight. They will peel like a charm. This works for red or yellow peppers, but not for green peppers.

# Onion-Tarragon Sauce

*Use sweet onions for this and the next sauce, and be sure to cook them slowly to develop their sweetness. If you make your own brown sauce, great, but you'll be surprised how good a canned beef gravy will taste when you doctor it up with fresh ingredients. (Check the ingredients and avoid brands that contain hydrolized vegetable protein.) This sauce is especially good for baked lamb shanks or roast pork.*

2 pounds sweet onions
2 tablespoons olive oil
½ cup red wine
3 tablespoons brandy
1½ cups brown sauce or 1 jar beef gravy
¼ cup tomato sauce
3 or 4 sprigs tarragon
Salt and freshly ground pepper

Peel the onions, cut them in half lengthwise, and cut off the roots and tips. Cut the onions lengthwise into 3 sections, then slice them crosswise to make thin strips about 1 inch long. (You can also chop the onions, but I like the look and feel of these strips.) In a large, wide saucepan or chicken fryer, heat the olive oil over moderate heat and cook the onions gently, without browning, until they are very soft, about 20 minutes. Stir them every now and then so they cook evenly.

Add the red wine and brandy. Boil the mixture until the liquid is reduced to about ¼ cup. Add the brown sauce, tomato sauce, and tarragon. Simmer for 10 to 15 minutes. Remove the tarragon sprigs and season to taste with salt and plenty of pepper. Makes enough for 6 to 8 servings.

# Walla Walla Basil Sauce

*I use this as a pasta sauce—it makes enough for 1 pound of pasta—but it can serve equally well anywhere you want the earthy sweetness of slow-cooked onions and the freshness of basil.*

Peel the onions, cut them in half, and slice them thin. In a wide, deep skillet or a dutch oven, toss the onions with the olive oil. Over medium heat, cook the onions until they begin to wilt, stirring them occasionally. Lower the heat and continue cooking the onions gently, stirring them occasionally, until they soften into a pale golden mass. They should not brown.

Now add the brandy and continue to cook and stir for another 15 to 20 minutes over low heat. All the liquid should evaporate. This recipe can be prepared in advance to this point.

Just before serving, pile the basil leaves on one another and slice them into thin strips. Stir them into the warm onion sauce with the salt and pepper. Makes enough sauce for 6 servings of pasta. Serve it with grated Parmesan.

8 to 10 Walla Walla sweet onions (5 pounds)
½ cup olive oil
¼ cup brandy
3 cups fresh basil leaves, lightly packed (no stems)
½ teaspoon salt
½ teaspoon freshly ground pepper
Grated Parmesan

Q. *Can all herbs be frozen?*

A. Yes, but although they keep their flavor beautifully, they tend to lose their color when you freeze them. Use frozen herbs only for flavoring. One efficient way to package big-leaf herbs such as basil for freezing is to leave the leaves on the stems and roll them up jelly roll style in plastic wrap. Tear off a long piece of plastic wrap and arrange the basil over it in a single layer. Roll it up and twist the ends to seal. Just unroll as much as you need and replace the rest in the freezer.

**Q.** *My basil plants are burgeoning. How do I make a simple pesto sauce?*

**A.** Herewith, my no-measure formula for making pesto sauce in a food processor: Pack the processor container with washed and dried leaves (no stems) up to the top of the knife handle. Add a handful of pine nuts and three to six peeled cloves of garlic. Add salt and freshly ground pepper to your taste. Start the machine. Scrape it down once or twice until the basil is very finely chopped. With the machine running, add enough olive oil to form a thick paste. Done.

Add freshly grated Parmesan cheese and more oil, if desired, when you use the pesto. This can be successfully frozen by spooning the pesto, without cheese, into ice cube trays. Each little container holds enough for one serving of pasta. Just thaw it out and toss it with the pasta, cheese and more oil, if desired.

# Avocado Pesto

*Avocado gives this pesto an elusive, almost buttery flavor that blends meltingly with pasta. Prepare it as close to serving time as possible, so it doesn't darken. With a food processor, the whole thing goes together in a flash.*

Cut the Parmesan into small pieces and place in the food processor fitted with the steel blade. Process for a minute or so, until cheese is pulverized. Drop in the avocado and garlic, and process until avocado is smooth, scraping down the bowl once or twice. Add the basil and continue processing until you have a fairly smooth mixture. With the machine running, slowly pour in the olive oil; the more you use, the thinner the sauce will become. Season to taste with salt and pepper, and scrape the sauce into a large serving bowl.

Toss with cooked pasta in the serving bowl, using a big spoon and fork and lifting the noodles or spaghetti high as you mix, so every strand is coated. Makes enough for 1 pound of pasta, or 4 to 6 servings.

4 ounces Parmesan
1 large, ripe avocado or 2 smaller ones, peeled and pitted
2 large cloves garlic, peeled
1 cup tightly packed fresh basil leaves (about 1 large bunch)
¼ to ½ cup olive oil
Salt and freshly ground pepper

# Tarragon Pesto

*This sauce is wonderful when you crave pesto out of season. Fresh hothouse tarragon is available year-round now. Basil, for some reason, remains highly seasonal.*

Remove and discard the stems from the spinach. Pick the tarragon leaves off their stems and discard those stems. Peel the garlic.

Place the spinach, tarragon and garlic in a food processor. Add the salt and a dash of pepper. Process until the ingredients are finely chopped, scraping down the sides of the bowl once or twice.

With the machine still running, add olive oil. Add the walnuts last. When the nuts are finely chopped, remove to a serving bowl. Makes enough for 1½ to 2 pounds of spaghetti, or 8 to 10 servings.

1 bunch spinach
½ cup fresh tarragon leaves
2 cloves garlic
1 teaspoon salt (or to taste)
Freshly ground pepper
⅓ to ½ cup olive oil
8 to 10 walnuts, or ⅓ cup pieces

# Chive Pesto

*This bright green sauce is sensational for pasta, rice, or baked potatoes. Fresh chives are inexpensive and plentiful, often easier to find than fresh basil, and certainly easier to grow for home gardeners. The blue cheese gives this pesto a creaminess most pestos don't have.*

3 or 4 large bunches (about 2 ounces) fresh chives
3 large cloves garlic, peeled
½ cup parsley sprigs
½ cup walnut pieces
½ teaspoon salt
½ to ¾ cup olive oil
4 ounces Stilton, Gorgonzola, or other blue cheese (about ½ cup mashed or finely crumbled)

In a food processor fitted with a steel blade, place the chives, garlic, parsley, walnut pieces, salt, and ½ cup of the olive oil. Process for several seconds, then stop and scrape down the sides. Process again until smooth. Add the cheese and whirl again until perfectly smooth and blended—about 20 seconds. If you wish, with the machine running, pour in the remaining olive oil. This isn't necessary; it just makes the sauce a little creamier and richer. Makes about 1¼ cups.

# Ginger Orange Sauce

Beurre blanc *sauces are often flavored with lemon, shallots, wine, and herbs. The flavors of this version—delicious on plain baked, steamed, or microwaved fish or scallops—are so concentrated that a little goes a very long way, and it really needs no salt or pepper.*

Combine the orange juice and vinegar in a small saucepan and reduce them over high heat to 2 tablespoons—the mixture becomes dark and syrupy. Watch carefully, so it doesn't evaporate entirely. Remove from heat and immediately swirl in 2 tablespoons of the butter. Continue to whisk in the remaining butter, 2 tablespoons at a time. Stir in the ginger. You may keep the sauce warm over faint heat, such as on the back of the stove or near a pilot light, for about 20 minutes, but if kept warm too long or reheated, it separates. Makes ⅔ cup.

½ cup fresh orange juice
1 tablespoon white wine vinegar or cider vinegar
8 tablespoons (1 stick) soft butter
2 teaspoons peeled and grated fresh ginger

**Q.** *I have been seeing a lot of wine labels that say, "contains sulfites." What are sulfites and should I be worried about them?*

**A.** All wines contain some sulfites. They always have. Some are produced naturally during fermentation. Some are added, in the form of sulfur dioxide, at the winery to prevent spoilage in the wine and help keep equipment clean. Too much sulfur dioxide gives the wine a taste like a burnt match. (Sulfur dioxide is, after all, the stuff produced when you burn sulfur, as in the tip of a match.) Wineries these days are using much less sulfur than ever, especially in the finest wines. But the government decided only in 1985 that wines ought to say on the label that they contain sulfites.

Those who are exquisitely sensitive to sulfur dioxide, some asthmatics in particular, should avoid wine. The rest of us are unaffected by the tiny amounts of sulfites in most wines, around 20 to 75 parts per million.

# Mint-Yogurt Mayonnaise

*The tartness of yogurt and sweetness of mint make a refreshing sauce for dressing salads, spreading on turkey sandwiches, or giving a lift to steamed vegetables.*

Ⅰn a blender or food processor, combine the mayonnaise, yogurt, and mint. Process the mixture until the mint is very finely chopped, then add lemon juice to taste. Makes 2 cups.

1 cup mayonnaise
½ cup plain yogurt
1 cup fresh mint leaves, packed
2 tablespoons lemon juice

# Low-fat Pepper Cream

*This low-fat sauce is wonderful on grilled fish, chicken, or pasta. To give it a little added zip, blend in a bit of Dijon mustard.*

Ⅰirst prepare the peppers. Use the Joe Carcione method to peel them: Place the peppers in a baking pan and put them in a 350-degree oven for 1 hour. Turn off the oven, cover the pan and let the peppers cool in the turned-off oven for 1 or 2 hours (or overnight). The peppers will peel easily. Discard the stems and seeds.

In a food processor, puree the cottage cheese. Stop the machine and scrape down the sides occasionally. Process the cheese until it is very smooth, 2 or 3 minutes. (This cream can be sweetened and used to garnish berry pies or used in place of high-fat Mascarpone.)

Add the peppers to the cheese puree. Blend until very smooth, about 30 seconds. Salt to taste. If you want to add a little more texture to the cream, peel, seed, and chop the tomato; transfer the pepper cream to a bowl and fold in the tomato. Do not puree the tomato or else the cream can become too watery.

2 red bell peppers or pimientos
1 pint (16 ounces) low-fat cottage
  cheese
1 medium tomato (optional)

**Q.** *How do I make sun-dried tomatoes? Can I make them in the oven?*

**A.** I'll never forget the first time I tasted a sun-dried tomato. It was at the Oakville Grocery, when it had a store in San Francisco. The grocery buyer offered me a taste of a new import from Italy. The heady, superconcentrated sweet taste of tomato was unforgettable. These tomatoes are also expensive, so I can understand why people want to make them at home.

If you have one, use a fruit drier. Just cut Roma tomatoes in half and sprinkle them lightly with salt. Arrange them on drying trays and put them in the drier. They are done when they feel leathery. It usually takes 6 to 10 hours.

Using the oven is trickier, but you can do the same job by arranging the tomatoes on cookie sheets. Turn the oven on to 200° F. for 10 minutes, then turn it off. Cycle the oven on and off once an hour until the tomatoes are dry enough. The process should take about eight hours.

# Cranberry-Pineapple Relish

*Have you noticed that modern cookbooks seem to have eliminated cranberry sauce from the repertoire? This is a refreshing change of pace from the usual cranberry-orange fare.*

Using a food processor, chop the cranberries, pineapple, and sugar with rapid pulses until the mixture is evenly chopped but not too fine. Turn it out into a bowl and mix in the grapefruit juice and liqueur. Serve it with almost anything that requires a bit of a jolt. Use it often. Refrigerated, it will keep for months, but it won't last that long. Makes 3½ to 4 cups.

1 package (12 ounces) whole cranberries
1½ cups chopped fresh pineapple
¾ cup sugar (preferably superfine)
¼ cup grapefruit juice
1 tablespoon orange liqueur (such as Cointreau, Grand Marnier, or triple sec)

---

# Whole Berry Cranberry Sauce

*My sister-in-law, who claims to hate cranberry sauce, lapped this up one Thanksgiving. Then we discovered that she really hated the tinny flavor of canned cranberry sauce. The whole ground orange contributes plenty of flavor.*

Combine the water and sugar in a saucepan. Boil the mixture for 5 minutes. Meanwhile, cut the orange or tangerine into eighths and remove the seeds. Grind the remaining portion (skin and pulp) or chop it fine in a food processor. Add the orange pulp and cranberries to the syrup. Boil the mixture for 5 minutes, or until the cranberries are soft and popping. Let the mixture cool before serving. This sauce will keep for several weeks in the refrigerator. Makes 4 cups.

1½ cups water
1½ cups sugar
12 ounces (1 package) whole fresh cranberries
1 small orange or tangerine

# Pineapple-Pepper Relish

*This is good with plain grilled chicken or firm-fleshed grilled fish. It is not terribly hot, because most of the heat in the jalapeño is in the seeds and membrane surrounding them.*

1 large ripe pineapple

1½ cups finely chopped bell pepper, red, green, or a combination

½ cup finely chopped red onion

1 small jalapeño pepper, seeded and minced

⅓ cup cider vinegar

2 tablespoons sugar

1 teaspoon salt

¼ cup chopped cilantro

Peel the pineapple, cutting deeply enough to remove the "eyes," then quarter it lengthwise. Cut the central core from each quarter, then chop the pineapple. Put the chopped fruit in a sieve or colander over a bowl and press out as much juice as you can; it makes a pleasant drink.

In a bowl, toss the drained pineapple with the bell pepper, red onion, and jalapeño. Add the vinegar, sugar, salt, and cilantro, toss well, and refrigerate for several hours, tossing occasionally. Drain before serving. Makes about 3 cups.

# Pesto Salad

*This is basically a parsley salad that grew up.*

Make the dressing by pureeing the garlic, olive oil, lemon juice, and salt and pepper in a blender or food processor. Set it aside.

Wash and dry the basil and parsley. Coarsely chop the basil, and toss it with the parsley, pine nuts, cheese, and the dressing. This dressing is best if it is made at least an hour in advance so the flavors meld. Makes 4 to 6 servings.

2 to 4 cloves garlic, peeled
½ cup olive oil
3 tablespoons lemon juice or 2 tablespoons vinegar
Salt and freshly ground pepper
½ to 1 cup basil leaves, loosely packed
4 cups (2 bunches) parsley sprigs
½ cup chopped pine nuts
½ cup grated Parmesan

# Spinach and Pear Salad

*This hearty salad is an especially luscious combination of flavors, colors and textures. The garnish of walnuts and Gorgonzola gives it enough heft to be a luncheon main course, or serve it in smaller portions as a dinnertime first course.*

2 large bunches (about 2 pounds)
   fresh spinach, large stems removed
2 large Bartlett pears
¼ cup olive oil
1 tablespoon red wine vinegar or
   balsamic vinegar
½ teaspoon salt
Freshly ground pepper
½ to 1 cup crumbled blue cheese
½ cup chopped walnuts

In a screw-topped jar, combine the oil, vinegar, salt, and pepper. Cap tightly, and shake vigorously until completely blended. Pour half the dressing over the spinach, toss, and arrange in a bed on a large platter.

Peel and core the pears. Slice them thin, pour the remaining dressing over them, toss, and arrange neatly over the spinach. Sprinkle the cheese and nuts on the top, and serve immediately. (Spinach wilts quickly when it has been tossed with the dressing.) Makes 4 servings.

# Pear and Grape Salad

*Some of the grapes are pureed and strained, and their juice is used in an unusual whipped cream vinaigrette, which is spooned over pears and grapes on a bed of curly endive, topped with crumbled blue cheese.*

Pull the grapes from the stems. Puree 1 cup of the grapes, then strain to extract the juice. Combine ¼ cup of the juice (if you have extra, drink it) with the vinegar and oil in a screw-topped jar. Season with salt and pepper, cap tightly, and shake vigorously to blend.

Toss ¼ cup of the dressing with the curly endive and arrange it on a large platter. Halve the remaining grapes—use a small, sharp knife and this chore goes very quickly—and toss with the pears. Spoon the fruit over the endive. In a small bowl, whip the cream until stiff, then fold in the remaining dressing. Spoon over the fruit and top with crumbled blue cheese. Makes 4 to 6 servings.

1 pound red seedless grapes
2 tablespoons cider vinegar
⅓ cup olive oil
Salt and freshly ground pepper
1 head escarole or curly endive, cleaned and torn in pieces
2 large pears, peeled, cored, and diced
⅓ cup whipping cream
1 cup (about 4 ounces) crumbled blue cheese (optional)

# Fennel and Radish Salad

*This cool, crunchy salad, with a delicate anise flavor and shreds of red radish, is best eaten within a few hours. If refrigerated overnight, it wilts and almost becomes more of a relish, although it is still good eating.*

1½ pounds fennel bulbs
2 bunches (about 30) red radishes
½ cup olive oil
3 tablespoons wine vinegar
½ teaspoon salt
Freshly ground pepper
2 tablespoons chopped parsley
Lettuce leaves or Belgian endive
   leaves

Trim the fennel and slice it very thin. Trim the radishes (don't peel them) and shred them—a food processor shredding disk is useful for this. Toss the fennel and radishes together. In a tightly capped jar, shake together the oil, vinegar, salt, and pepper. Pour over the vegetables and toss to combine. Let sit for 1 or 2 hours, tossing occasionally. Just before serving, toss in the parsley, and mound the salad on lettuce or endive leaves. Makes 4 to 6 servings.

# Grapefruit and Tomato Salad

*Even in the middle of winter, we can still have a bright, summery salad. The dressing is especially light—because it's made with grapefruit juice instead of vinegar.*

Peel the grapefruit with a small, sharp knife, removing all the white covering and exposing the bright red flesh all around. Now cut between each membrane, letting the whole grapefruit sections fall into a bowl. Cut each cherry tomato in half. Cut the Belgian endive crosswise into ½-inch thick slices. Remove any large, tough stems from the watercress.

Spread the pieces of endive in a thin layer on a large serving platter. Arrange the grapefruit sections around the circumference, then drop the tomato halves between and around the grapefruit. Pile the watercress in the center of the platter, making a large, green bouquet—in fact, the whole arrangement looks like a giant flower in bloom. Combine the grapefruit juice, oil, salt, and pepper in a screw-topped jar, cap tightly, and shake vigorously to blend. Drizzle over the salad and serve immediately. Makes 4 servings.

**2 large ruby red grapefruit**
**1 cup red or yellow cherry tomatoes**
**1 large head Belgian endive**
**1 large bunch watercress**
**3 tablespoons grapefruit juice**
**⅓ cup olive oil**
**Salt and freshly ground pepper**

# Parsnip and Celery Root Salad

*Another variation on the sweet-and-earthy flavor theme, this salad pairs the sweetness of parsnips and green onion with the celery root to make a lovely salad.*

1 pound celery root
1 pound parsnips
⅔ cup mayonnaise
½ cup sour cream
¼ cup chopped green onion
2 tablespoons cider vinegar
1 teaspoon dried tarragon
½ teaspoon salt
½ teaspoon freshly ground pepper

Peel the celery root and parsnips, and shred them with the coarse disk of the food processor, or cut them by hand into very fine julienne. Blend together the remaining ingredients. Add to the vegetables and toss to combine thoroughly. Chill for a few hours before serving, then toss well again, adding more salt and pepper if necessary. Makes 6 to 8 servings.

---

Q. *How far in advance can I boil potatoes for potato salad?*

A. Potatoes absorb more flavor if they are mixed with the dressing while they are still warm. That is why potato salad recipes call for peeling and cutting the potatoes "as soon as they are cool enough to handle." If you cannot make up the salad right away, at least toss the potatoes with some oil, vinegar, and seasonings. The salad will taste better. Once dressed, most potato salads can be held one or two days in the refrigerator without harm.

# Mustardy Potato Salad

*Everybody likes the bacon and mustard flavor of this potato salad. Try it on your next picnic. Use thin-skinned boiling potatoes such as red Bliss or white Rose, which maintain their texture, rather than thicker-skinned baking potatoes, which turn mealy when cooked. I prefer to leave the potato skins on, but feel free to peel them if you would rather.*

Wash the potatoes and put them in a saucepan of cold water with 1 tablespoon salt. Bring them to a boil and let them simmer until they are tender, about 15 to 20 minutes.

Meanwhile, remove strings from the celery and cut it into fine dice. Slice the green onions fairly thin, about ⅛ to ¼ inch. Chop the herbs—sage and oregano are especially good. Cook the bacon in a skillet or microwave oven until it is crisp. Crumble the bacon. Combine these ingredients with the dressing or mayonnaise in a large mixing bowl.

When the potatoes are done, drain them well. Leave them in the saucepan and place it under cold running water. When the potatoes are cool enough to handle, but still warm, cut them into bite-size chunks (about ¾-inch square by ½-inch thick) and add them to the bowl containing the dressing.

Spoon the mustard onto the warm potatoes. Stir it around, season with salt and pepper to taste, and fold the potatoes and the dressing together until well combined. Season with salt and pepper to taste. Let stand 15 to 20 minutes before serving, if possible, for flavors to blend. Makes 6 to 8 servings.

**1¼ pounds thin-skinned potatoes**
**2 ribs celery**
**4 green onions**
**1 tablespoon fresh herbs of your choice (see below)**
**4 strips bacon**
**½ cup White Cloud Dressing (page 178) or mayonnaise**
**2 heaping tablespoons Dijon mustard**

# Mashed Potato Salad

*A couple of friends scoffed at this, then ate most of the bowl. It's a little lighter than a traditional potato salad, because it's made without mayonnaise. The taste is reminiscent of classic American potato salad, with the good flavor of potatoes, green onion, vinegar, and olive oil.*

2 ½ pounds (about 5) thin-skinned
  potatoes
1 teaspoon salt
½ teaspoon freshly ground pepper
6 tablespoons cider vinegar
½ cup olive oil
½ cup chopped green onion
¼ cup chopped parsley
2 hard-cooked eggs, peeled and
  chopped

Boil the potatoes in their jackets until tender when pierced, then drain. When still quite warm, but just cool enough to handle, peel them and drop in a large bowl. Sprinkle with the salt and pepper and mash slightly. Add the vinegar gradually as you mash more vigorously. Continue mashing as you add the olive oil—some small lumps should remain; it needn't be perfectly smooth. Stir in the green onion, parsley, and eggs. The salad is delicious now, while slightly warm, at room temperature, or chilled. Makes 8 to 10 servings.

# Potato Salad with Smoked Salmon-Caper Dressing

*Boiled potatoes, dill, capers, olive oil, and lemon juice are traditional accompaniments for smoked salmon. They also make an unusual potato salad. The mayonnaise dressing can be made easily in the food processor.*

Boil the potatoes in salted water until they are just tender when pierced. Drain and let cool to room temperature. Peel them if you wish—many people like to leave the skins on. When cool, cut into ½-inch dice, and drop them in a bowl.

In a food processor, combine the egg yolks, lemon juice, and mustard and whirl for 30 seconds. With the machine running, slowly pour in the olive oil; the mixture will emulsify into a thick, creamy mayonnaise. Season well with pepper and lightly with salt (the smoked salmon to come later is salty itself.) Add the dill sprigs and process until they are chopped throughout the mayonnaise. Add the capers and salmon and process in quick pulses, just until they are blended into the sauce—the fish should remain in about ½-inch pieces. Taste and add more lemon juice or seasoning if you wish. Toss the diced potatoes with the mayonnaise and refrigerate until serving. Makes 6 servings.

2½ pounds (5 to 8) red-skinned potatoes
2 egg yolks
2 tablespoons (or more) lemon juice
2 teaspoons Dijon mustard
⅔ cup olive oil
Salt and freshly ground pepper
½ cup (loosely packed) fresh dill sprigs
1 tablespoon capers
3 to 4 ounces smoked salmon

# Hot Cabbage and Pepper Slaw

*Cole slaw today is most often made with a mayonnaise, sour cream, or vinaigrette dressing. But an old-fashioned boiled dressing—popular before commercial mayonnaise was so common—is more traditional. When you pour it hot over the shredded cabbage and peppers, they will wilt slightly, absorb the dressing and become quite pungent with the flavor. The slaw is especially good with fish or baked ham.*

1 cabbage (about 1½ pounds)
2 red or green bell peppers
2 tablespoons butter
2 tablespoons flour
½ cup water
6 tablespoons sugar
3 egg yolks
1 teaspoon salt
½ cup cider vinegar

Core and shred the cabbage. Seed and thinly slice the peppers. Mix them together in a large bowl; set aside.

Melt the butter in a heavy-bottom saucepan; stir in the flour and cook a minute or two without browning. Whisk in the water and continue cooking until mixture thickens and boils. Remove from heat and beat in the sugar, egg yolks, and salt. Return to heat and boil gently, stirring constantly, for 1 minute more. Whisk in the vinegar, then pour over the cabbage mixture. Toss to coat thoroughly. Best served warm but may also be served chilled. Makes 6 to 8 servings.

# Warm Radicchio and Pepper Slaw

*Radicchio looks like a little cabbage, but it has a bite of its own that plays nicely off the sweetness of the bell peppers and apple. Equally good warm or at room temperature, this dish goes well with all kinds of roast meats and poultry or with French bread and a wedge of goat cheese.*

Cut the peppers in half. Scoop out the seeds and cut the peppers into thin strips. Halve and core the apple (don't peel it) then shred on the large holes of a grater. Squeeze firmly by handfuls to remove as much juice as you can from the grated apple. Drink or discard the juice. Core and finely shred the radicchio; there should be about 3 cups.

In a large, heavy skillet, heat the oil until it is almost smoking. Throw in the peppers and apple, and toss and stir briskly over high heat for a minute or two—just until the peppers are glistening and bright, but still slightly crunchy. Add the vinegar and sugar and toss a few more seconds. Remove from heat and immediately add the radicchio and salt, tossing well to mix. Turn out onto a platter. Makes 4 servings.

3 bell peppers (red, green, yellow, or a mixture)
1 large firm apple (Pippin or Golden Delicious)
1 medium to large head radicchio
2 tablespoons olive oil
3 tablespoons red wine vinegar or cider vinegar
1 tablespoon sugar
½ teaspoon salt

# Avocado Dressing

*Oil-rich avocado makes a rich, smooth emerald-green dressing that requires no additional oil. Use it on any green salad.*

1 large ripe avocado (about 6 ounces)
2 green onions, trimmed
Juice of ½ lemon
2 tablespoons chopped parsley or
    basil
¾ teaspoon salt
Freshly ground black pepper
¾ cup buttermilk, or more to taste

Combine all the ingredients except the buttermilk in a food processor or blender. Blend until smooth, then add the buttermilk and blend. Add enough buttermilk to make a mixture about the texture of thick cream. Makes 1½ to 2 cups.

# C. K.'s Salad Dressing

*C. K.'s is the restaurant at the Tampa Airport hotel. When it opened in 1974 with a team of chefs from the Culinary Institute of America, it overnight became the best airport restaurant in the United States and a destination restaurant for Tampans. The salad dressing was especially intriguing, and when I shared it on the "KCBS Kitchen" it was a smash. It is the best cream-style dressing I know.*

Blend all the ingredients well. Taste the dressing for salt and other seasonings. Makes 4 cups.

*Note:* To make fresh cracked pepper, wrap the peppercorns in wax paper. Fold the edges carefully to seal, then hit them with a hammer until all the peppercorns are cracked.

2½ cups mayonnaise (made without olive oil)
1 cup sour cream
1 tablespoon chopped fresh dill or 1½ teaspoons dried
3 tablespoons grated Parmesan
2½ teaspoons cracked pepper
1 clove garlic
Juice of ½ lemon
1 tablespoon Worcestershire sauce
2 teaspoons grated onion
2 teaspoons cider vinegar

# Green Goddess Dressing

*As long as we're having a vogue for "California Cuisine," why not go back to one of the great recipes to come from California? This salad dressing was created at the Garden Court at the Palace Hotel around the turn of the century.*

1 clove garlic
8 to 10 anchovies
1 green onion
¼ cup parsley leaves
2 tablespoons fresh tarragon leaves
   or 2 teaspoons dried
3 cups mayonnaise
¼ cup vinegar (preferably tarragon
   vinegar)
¼ cup chopped chives

Cut the clove of garlic in half and rub the inside of the mixing bowl with it. Mash the anchovies in the bowl. Chop the green onion and parsley and add it to the bowl, along with the tarragon. Blend in the mayonnaise and vinegar. Fold in the chives. Makes about 4 cups. This keeps in the refrigerator about 3 to 4 weeks in a tightly covered container.

# Cream "Mayonnaise" Dressing

*Your grandmother may have made "mayonnaise" somewhat like this way back in 1912. It was a popular sauce in Europe, useful as a sandwich spread, and also delicious spooned over cold poached fish. The flavor is between "real" mayonnaise and a good egg salad. If you wish, you can also fold in the chopped hard-boiled egg whites. For cholesterol-watchers, try the White Cloud Dressing (page 178).*

Place the egg yolks in a bowl and mash them with a fork or spoon. Add the salt, pepper, mustard, and lemon juice, mashing and blending again until smooth. Add the cream and beat with an electric or hand-held rotary beater until the sauce begins to thicken—the longer you beat, the thicker it will become. It should be soft and spreadable for sandwiches, less thick for spooning over fish. If the dressing becomes too thick, thin it with a tablespoon or so of milk. Fold in the capers or relish. Chill until serving. Makes about 2 cups. This will keep for about 2 weeks.

4 hard-boiled egg yolks
½ teaspoon salt
¼ teaspoon freshly ground pepper
2 teaspoons mustard, yellow or Dijon
1 tablespoon lemon juice
⅔ cup heavy whipping cream
2 tablespoons chopped capers or pickle relish or a combination

# White Cloud Dressing

*This is an old-fashioned variation on mayonnaise. Only the egg whites are used, which is just the ticket for cholesterol watchers. It makes an especially light and fluffy sauce, with or without a food processor.*

2 egg whites
2 tablespoons vinegar
1 teaspoon salt
Pinch of white pepper
¾ cup vegetable oil
⅓ cup buttermilk or milk

Put the egg whites and vinegar in a food processer fitted with the metal blade. Process until meringue forms (about 20 seconds). Blend in the salt and pepper.

With motor running, pour in the oil, then blend in the milk. The dressing should be the consistency of very thick cream. It can be thinned with milk or cream. Use like mayonnaise as a salad dressing, or flavor it as you would mayonnaise.

Without a food processor, beat the egg whites in a clean bowl with a hand mixer or whisk until they form soft peaks. Blend in the vinegar, salt, and pepper. While beating, add the oil in a very thin stream until it is incorporated. Thin with milk to desired consistency. Makes 1¼ cups.

# Spiral Salad Dressing

*The Spiral was a vegetarian restaurant in Coral Gables, Florida, in the heyday of the bean sprouts and brown rice era. It served great vegetable tempura and a salad with an unusually flavorful dressing. This is my version. Light miso is a soy product available in Japanese and health food stores.*

Combine all the ingredients in a blender. Process the mixture until it is smooth and a little foamy. Keep it refrigerated. Makes 4½ cups.

*Note:* If *tamari* (a form of Japanese soy sauce) or light soy is not available, you may substitute ordinary soy sauce. The dressing will be darker. If rice wine vinegar is not available, use white wine vinegar.

2 cups vegetable oil
¾ cup light miso
¼ cup *tamari* sauce or light soy sauce
¼ cup rice wine vinegar
¾ cup water
¼ cup chopped onions
2 or 3 tablespoons honey

# Oil-free Mustard-Miso Dressing

*This low-calorie salad dressing gets its texture from the main ingredients and an egg yolk.*

2 teaspoons mustard powder
2 teaspoons cold water
1 egg yolk
2 teaspoons white miso
2 teaspoons soy sauce
1 tablespoon fresh lemon juice
1 tablespoon rice wine vinegar
2 tablespoons minced green onions
(white part only)

Mix the mustard powder and water together to form a thin paste. Allow it to sit for 10 minutes. Vigorously mix the egg yolk with the mustard. Then stir in the remaining ingredients in order listed, and allow to sit at least 10 minutes before use. Makes enough for a salad of 4 servings.

# Mustard-Honey Dressing

*While dining at Chateau St. Jean in Sonoma, I was struck by the flavors of this delicious dressing. The secret, from Bea Beasley of Bea Beasley and Co., turned out to be a blend of good-flavored oils and lots of parsley. This makes a large quantity, about 4 cups, but it keeps nicely in the refrigerator for weeks.*

Beat together all ingredients except oils, salt and pepper, and honey. Combine the oils and slowly add them in a steady stream, beating well. Add salt and pepper to taste. Fold honey into the dressing. Makes about 4 cups.

2 tablespoons Dijon mustard
¼ cup onion, minced
1 cup flat-leafed parsley, minced
1 clove garlic, peeled and minced
1 egg
3 tablespoons soy sauce
¾ cup red wine vinegar
1½ cups peanut oil
¼ cup Oriental sesame oil
½ cup olive oil
Salt and freshly ground pepper
½ cup honey

# Sautéed Cucumbers with Dill

*This is a great last-minute vegetable dish, especially good with salmon prepared any way you like. It is also good with chicken or prawns.*

1 large cucumber or 2 medium
2 teaspoons salt
2 tablespoons butter
1 shallot or ¼ onion, minced
1 tablespoon fresh chopped dill or 1
   teaspoon dried
½ cup sour cream (optional)

Peel the cucumber; if it is the American type, cut it in half lengthwise and scoop out the seeds. Using the grater blade in a food processor, cut the cucumbers in julienne strips. This can also be done on a mandoline or by hand. If cutting by hand, it is easier to make thin slices instead of julienne. Salt the cucumber and let it drain in a bowl or in a colander for 30 minutes. Rinse well.

In a skillet, melt the butter and sauté the shallot or onion gently for 1 minute, or until it is soft. Add the cucumber, raise the heat and sauté it for 3 to 5 minutes, or until it is limp but not falling apart. Sprinkle it with dill and, if you want a creamy dish, stir in the sour cream. After adding the cream, do not let it boil. Makes 6 servings.

# Grilled Marinated Vegetables

*Whenever you've fired up the barbecue grill for chicken, fish, or steaks, use the first heat of the coals to grill vegetables as a side dish or appetizer. Japanese eggplant works especially well. So do bell peppers of all kinds (especially red or yellow), squashes, and onions (red or green). "Hard" vegetables such as broccoli or green beans are poor choices.*

To prepare the vegetables: Cut Japanese eggplants in half lengthwise. Cut larger eggplant, zucchini and squashes into ½-inch slices, crosswise or lengthwise. Cut peppers into halves lengthwise, large peppers into fourths. Green onions should be left whole. Red onions should be cut lengthwise into ½-inch slices. They hold together better that way.

Blend the marinade ingredients with a fork or spoon. Paint the marinade on the vegetables as they cook on the grill. Turn them several times until they brown evenly. Brush any remaining marinade on the vegetables after they come off the grill. Serve warm or at room temperature. Makes enough for 2 pounds of vegetables, or 4 to 6 servings.

**Marinade:**
½ cup olive oil
1 tablespoon soy sauce (mushroom flavored soy is good)
1 tablespoon sherry wine vinegar
¼ teaspoon white pepper

# Layered Vegetables Provençal

*The ingredients are essentially those of ratatouille, except they are arranged differently to make a fresher-tasting side dish.*

1 clove garlic
¼ to ½ cup olive oil
2 shallots or 1 small onion
4 large ripe tomatoes
4 zucchini, about 1 inch thick
4 Chinese or Japanese eggplants
Salt and freshly ground pepper
Allspice
Grated Parmesan or bread crumbs

Rub the bottom of a 9 × 13-inch baking pan with the cut garlic clove. Drizzle in enough olive oil to coat the bottom. Spread it with a spatula or paper towel if necessary.

Finely chop the shallots or onions. Put them in a clean towel and squeeze them dry. This squeezes out the harsh flavor. Sprinkle the shallots over the bottom of the pan.

Preheat the oven to 375° F.

Peel the tomatoes and slice them lengthwise as thin as possible, about ¼ inch or less. Cut the zucchini diagonally the same thickness and likewise the eggplant. Arrange the vegetables in overlapping rows to fill the baking pan. Sprinkle them with salt, pepper, and a pinch of allspice (or nutmeg).

Bake the vegetables for 15 minutes, then sprinkle them with the cheese or bread crumbs. Bake a few minutes longer to brown the surface lightly. Cut into squares or rectangles and lift them out with a wide spatula to serve. Makes 6 to 8 servings.

*Note:* It is easy to increase or decrease this recipe to provide more servings in a larger pan or fewer in a smaller pan. Some people prefer to make 2 layers of vegetables, one on top of the other, for a thicker serving.

# Smoky Spinach

*This bright green sauté of spinach has both Chinese and American overtones. The preliminary cooking of the spinach can be completed way ahead, and the final cooking requires just a heating through to blend the flavors. Serve with barbecued chicken, ribs, or hamburgers.*

Remove any long stems from the washed spinach—don't worry about removing the smaller, tender stems. Place in a large kettle, cover, and cook over medium heat for about 10 minutes, stirring occasionally, just until spinach is wilted. Remove from heat, drain well, and flood the spinach with lots of cold water to cool it and stop the cooking. Drain well again, squeezing it by handfuls to remove as much water as possible.

Cook the bacon until crisp; drain slices and crumble them.

Just before serving, heat the olive and sesame oils in a skillet until quite hot. Toss in the spinach, then stir and toss for 2 or 3 minutes, until spinach is coated with oil and heated through. Add the bourbon and soy sauce and stir and toss for about 2 minutes more. Add the bacon, toss to distribute it throughout the spinach, and serve. Serves 6 to 8 as a side dish.

**6 bunches spinach (2 ½ to 3 pounds before cleaning)**
**2 tablespoons olive oil**
**1 tablespoon Oriental sesame oil**
**3 tablespoons bourbon**
**3 tablespoons soy sauce**
**6 slices bacon**

# Sauté of Spinach and Spaghetti Squash

*A cooked spaghetti squash separates into long, golden pastalike threads, and the lovely strands with a subtle squash flavor are a good foil for many additions and seasonings. Spinach and Parmesan not only make it colorful—gold flecked with dark green—but also make it taste amazingly like spaghetti, without a lot of the calories. The whole dish can be completed a day in advance, then tossed in a skillet for several minutes to reheat before serving.*

1 spaghetti squash (about 3 pounds)
2 large bunches spinach, large stems removed
3 tablespoons butter or olive oil
1 teaspoon salt
½ teaspoon freshly ground pepper
½ to 1 cup grated Parmesan

Put an inch or two of water in a large kettle, puncture the squash with a knife in several places to keep it from exploding, and place it on a rack above the water, then cover tightly. Bring to a boil and steam for about 30 minutes, just until the shell of the squash gives to moderate pressure from your finger. Cut open lengthwise, then scoop out the seeds and fibers from the centers. (Protect your hand with a pot holder or towel; the squash is hot.) Don't scoop down too forcefully, or you'll scrape out the flesh. With all the seeds out, scrape with a large fork, and the flesh will separate into "spaghetti."

Heat the butter or oil in a large skillet. Toss in the spinach and cook for several minutes, until wilted. Raise heat to high to evaporate excess moisture. Add the spaghetti squash and season with salt and pepper. Toss and stir for several minutes to heat through. This part may be done a day in advance. Just before serving, reheat and then toss in the Parmesan. Makes 6 to 8 servings.

# Corn Stew

*When fresh corn is in season, after you have had your fill of buttered corn on the cob, try this quick sauté as a light first course or something to serve around roast chicken.*

Peel, seed, and dice the tomatoes if fresh. In a large saucepan or deep skillet, gently sauté the onion and peppers in the butter until they are soft.

Meanwhile, cut the kernels from the corn into a bowl, scraping the milky juice from the cobs as well. When the onion is soft, add the corn to the onion-pepper mixture along with the tomatoes. Stir and cook for a minute, then add the milk, salt, and pepper. Simmer the mixture for 10 minutes. Finally, stir in the cilantro.

To make soup, add more milk or cream. For a side dish, use less milk or cream. As a flavor variation, omit the peppers and cilantro and add 2 dozen basil leaves. Makes 6 to 8 servings.

4 medium to large tomatoes or 1½ to 2 cups canned diced tomatoes
1 large onion, diced
1 bell pepper, diced
3 to 4 mild green chilies, finely chopped or use a 4-ounce can
1 jalapeño pepper, finely chopped (optional)
3 tablespoons butter
6 ears corn or 4 cups kernels
2 cups milk or half-and-half
Salt and freshly ground pepper
Cilantro leaves

# My Mother's Squash

*When I first started cooking for myself, I spent a lot of time on the phone asking my mother to describe to me just exactly how she prepared certain dishes that were favorites. How many kids like squash? This kid did, when my mother prepared it this way.*

1 pound yellow squash cut in ½- to ⅓-inch slices (about 3 cups)

½ pound onion (preferably red) cut in ⅛-inch slices (about 1 cup)

½ pound mushrooms cut in ⅓-inch slices (about 2 cups)

2 tablespoons chopped parsley

Salt and freshly ground pepper

2 tablespoons butter

Combine the vegetables in a saucepan large enough to hold them comfortably (about 3 quarts or larger). Add about 1 inch of water, the parsley, salt, and pepper to taste. Boil the vegetables for 5 minutes, or until the squash is barely cooked. Remove the vegetables with a slotted spoon and drain them well.

Boil the liquid remaining in the saucepan until it reduces to about 2 or 3 tablespoons. Swirl in the butter and pour it over the well-drained vegetables. Makes 6 to 8 servings.

# Baked Squash

*This simple and homey preparation of winter squash is especially good with roast chicken or squab. Solid-flesh squash, such as Hubbard, butternut or banana squash, perform better than stringy varieties, such as acorn.*

Preheat the oven to 375°F.

Peel and seed the squash, then cut it into ¾-inch cubes. If it didn't come in slices, cut the *pancetta* into thin slices. Season the squash with pepper and combine it in a large baking pan with the *pancetta* or bacon, broth, and cream or milk. Bake the squash for 30 minutes.

Uncover the pan, top the squash with bread crumbs and Parmesan, and bake it for 15 minutes longer, or until the top is brown and the liquid has nearly all evaporated. Makes 6 to 8 servings. It's also great reheated.

2 pounds winter squash
2 ounces *pancetta* or 3 slices bacon
Freshly ground pepper
1 cup chicken broth
¼ cup whipping cream or milk
⅓ cup bread crumbs
⅓ cup grated Parmesan

# Maple Butternut Squash

*Tender slivers of butternut squash, gently stewed and glazed with a little maple syrup, make a bright golden vegetable dish with a sweet-nutty flavor, to accompany all kinds of roast fowl or game.*

1 medium-size butternut squash
   (about 2 to 2½ pounds)
6 tablespoons (¾ stick) butter
½ teaspoon salt
¼ teaspoon freshly ground pepper
¼ cup maple syrup
¼ cup chopped pecans
2 tablespoons chopped parsley

Cut the stem end from the squash, then peel the squash, halve it and scoop out the seeds. Cut lengthwise into long strips about 1 inch wide, then slice the strips into quarter-size pieces about ⅛-inch thick.

Melt the butter in a large skillet over medium heat. Add the squash, toss well, then cover and let stew for about 5 to 10 minutes—the pieces of squash should be just tender when pierced, not mushy or falling apart; they will cook more later. (This step may be completed hours in advance; set aside partially covered until you are ready to continue.)

About 10 minutes before serving, reheat the squash until it sizzles. Sprinkle with the salt and pepper and pour on the maple syrup. Cook over moderate heat, tossing frequently for several minutes, until much of the liquid has evaporated and the squash is glazed with the butter and syrup. Sprinkle on the pecans and parsley, toss again, then turn into a warm vegetable dish. Makes 6 to 8 servings.

# Marinated Broiled Squash

*This simple herbed vegetable accompaniment or first course can be cooked partially ahead of time and finished just before serving, or cooked fully ahead of time and served at room temperature.*

Wash the squash, trim off the ends, then cut squash in half lengthwise. Place the halves in a large bowl and add the olive oil, herb, lemon zest, and several grinds of fresh pepper. (Don't add salt yet; it "cooks" the squash by drawing out the liquid.) Toss well to combine, and let sit for at least 30 minutes—or up to a couple of hours—tossing occasionally.

Preheat the broiler to red hot. Sprinkle the salt over the squash and toss well. Arrange in a single layer, skin-side-up, in a shallow broiling pan, reserving the oil left in the bowl. Place about 4 inches from heat and broil about 10 minutes, until lightly browned. Then turn cut-side-up and brush with some of the oil remaining in the bowl. (Set squash aside until you're ready to finish cooking, or complete cooking now, and serve them at room temperature.) Return to the hot broiler and cook 5 to 10 minutes longer, just until lightly browned. Makes 4 to 6 servings.

2 pounds (about 8 to 10) small (but not baby) summer squash, such as zucchini, crookneck, or pattypan
¼ cup olive oil
1 teaspoon dried basil or Italian seasoning
Finely grated zest of 1 lemon
Freshly ground pepper
½ teaspoon salt

# Scalloped Chayote

*The chayote, or mirliton, is a neglected vegetable, shaped like a big, green gnarly pear. Its plain flavor resembles zucchini, but the texture is much firmer and able to withstand long baking without becoming mushy or watery. It is delicious scalloped, like potatoes, and it can bake in the oven right along with whatever meat you're roasting. If you wish to make this a main course, throw in some thinly sliced or chopped leftover ham as you layer the casserole.*

3 large chayotes
4 tablespoons (¼ cup) butter
¼ cup flour
2 cups milk
Salt and freshly ground pepper to
    taste
1 cup toasted bread crumbs
½ cup shredded Cheddar

Preheat the oven to 350° F.

Butter a baking dish of about 2½-quart capacity.

Halve the chayotes and cut the pit from the center of each half. Cut the pitted chayotes into slices about ⅛-inch thick—use a food processor if you wish.

Melt the butter in a small pan, add the flour, and cook for a moment, then whisk in the milk. Bring to a boil, stirring, then season with salt and pepper to taste. Spread several spoonfuls of the sauce over the bottom of the prepared dish and sprinkle with ⅓ cup of the crumbs. Cover with half the chayote slices, then with half the remaining sauce and another ⅓ cup of the crumbs. Add the remaining chayote, spread with the last of the sauce, and sprinkle with the remaining crumbs.

Bake for about 1 hour, then sprinkle with the cheese and bake for about 30 minutes more, or until the chayote is tender when pierced, not mushy. Total baking time is about 1½ hours. Makes 6 servings.

# Broccoli and Mushrooms in Wine

*Theoretically, cooking green vegetables in wine should bleach their color, but something magical happens with this technique and everything comes out beautifully. Maybe it's the mushrooms.*

In a large, deep skillet or saucepan, heat the olive oil and sauté the garlic and mushrooms in the oil for 2 minutes. Discard the garlic and let the mushrooms cook for another minute, until they brown lightly. Add the broccoli, tossing quickly to coat each piece with the oil. Add the wine and salt and pepper to taste. Cook the broccoli in the wine, stirring it occasionally, for 3 minutes, then cover the pan and let the broccoli cook in the wine until it is tender, 2 to 5 minutes longer.

Remove the broccoli to a serving bowl, and turn up the heat to reduce the liquid by half. Pour the light sauce over the broccoli, and serve it with roast chicken or roast lamb—or any time you want a simple green vegetable. Makes 4 to 6 servings.

**3 tablespoons olive oil**
**2 cloves garlic, lightly crushed**
**¼ pound mushrooms, finely chopped**
**1 bunch broccoli, cut into florets**
**1½ cups dry white wine**
**Salt and freshly ground pepper**

---

**Q.** *Do those gold medal stickers on a bottle of wine mean anything?*

**A.** At one time they did, but now there are so many ways wines can legitimately win awards, you must look carefully at the fine print. (Besides, no laws restrict a winery from printing up a bunch of stickers and putting them on its wines.) At their best, wine competitions can identify lesser known wines that are worth seeking out. If there is a wine competition in your locality, try some of the wines that win and see if you agree. You might find something great you might not otherwise have tried.

---

# Brussels Sprouts with Potato and Chestnut

*The combination of flavors is delightful, with the sweet chestnut balancing the slight bitterness of the Brussels sprouts. The potato adds further balance. The recipe is from Kelly Mills, chef of the Four Seasons Clift Hotel.*

¾ pound Brussels sprouts
1 pound potatoes, peeled
¾ pound chestnuts
1 cup chicken stock
1 tablespoon butter

Cut the Brussels sprouts in half lengthwise. Using a ½-inch melon baller, cut the potatoes into balls. Cut the shells of the chestnuts with a sharp knife, then braise them in the chicken stock about 30 minutes. When they are cool, peel them.

Cook the sprouts in boiling water. When barely tender, immerse them in ice water to preserve their color. Boil the potato balls for 5 minutes, then sauté them golden in butter or oil. Heat the vegetables together in a skillet before serving. Makes 4 to 6 servings.

# Glazed Baked Onions

*Blanched then baked slowly in a sweet-sour glaze, these small onions are delicious with ribs or grilled sausages.*

Preheat the oven to 350° F.

Blanch the onions in boiling salted water for several minutes, until just tender when pierced. They are easy to peel at this point. Meanwhile, stir together the remaining ingredients. Drain the onions well and spread them in an 8-inch square baking dish. Pour on the honey mixture, stir to coat, and bake for about 1 hour, stirring occasionally, until the liquid has reduced to a syrupy glaze. Watch them carefully the last 15 minutes or so; they can burn easily. Serve them hot or at room temperature. Makes 4 to 6 servings.

1 pound boiling onions
3 tablespoons honey
3 tablespoons ketchup
2 tablespoons cider vinegar
2 tablespoons water
Pinch salt
Freshly ground pepper

# Spinach and Watercress Timbales

*Timbales—really a fancy custard—are a terrific way to use up leftover cooked meats and vegetables, without them appearing as such. These dark green timbales of spinach and peppery watercress are a delicious luncheon dish or a good vegetable accompaniment for any roast meat or poultry. They are also good picnic food, served cold, with mayonnaise.*

2 bunches spinach (about 1½ pounds)

2 bunches watercress (about ¾ pound)

3 tablespoons butter

½ cup fine, dry bread crumbs

1 cup beef or chicken broth

4 eggs at room temperature

⅔ cups grated Parmesan

With a sharp knife, cut off the tough stem ends of both the spinach and watercress bunches. Wash the leaves well in cold water. Steam them together for about 5 minutes in a covered kettle, using just the water that clings to the leaves, until completely wilted. Drain well, flood with cold water to stop the cooking, then drain again. Squeeze the vegetables a handful at a time to remove excess water, then puree in a food processor—you will have about 1¼ cups of puree.

Preheat the oven to 350° F.

Lightly butter 8 ramekins or custard cups. In a medium saucepan, combine and bring to a boil the butter, bread crumbs, and broth. Remove from heat. In a bowl, beat together the eggs, cheese, and vegetable puree. Beat this into the broth mixture. Spoon into the prepared molds, using about ⅓ cup for each. Set in a pan of hot water that comes about two-thirds of the way up the sides of the molds. Bake for 20 to 25 minutes, until set and lightly puffed.

Let cool 5 minutes, then run a knife around the inside of the cup, and unmold onto a warm platter or plates. Makes 8 timbales, enough for 4 to 8 servings.

# Rutabaga and Mushroom Puree

*In this good autumn vegetable dish, an earthy, golden puree of rutabaga is flecked with buttery mushroom duxelles, a sort of hash made by sautéing finely chopped mushrooms in butter until they are very brown.*

Chop the mushrooms very fine, stems and all. Melt 3 tablespoons of the butter in a heavy skillet. Add the mushrooms and cook over low heat, stirring occasionally, for about 30 minutes, until all the moisture has evaporated. Season with salt and pepper.

Cook the rutabagas in boiling salted water to cover until tender when pierced—about 45 minutes. Drain well and puree in a food processor with the remaining 2 tablespoons of butter and the milk or cream; if necessary, add a little more milk or cream to make a smooth puree. Stir the mushrooms into the puree and reheat in a double boiler (or a microwave oven) before serving. Makes 6 to 8 servings.

1 pound mushrooms
5 tablespoons butter
Salt and freshly ground pepper
3 rutabagas, peeled
6 or more tablespoons milk or cream

# Celery-Pear Puree

*Fruits and vegetables usually aren't pureed together, but this surprisingly delicious mixture with slightly sweet overtones is good with chicken, turkey, duck, or any other fowl.*

2 celery roots (about 1½ pounds)
1 tablespoon lemon juice
2 large Bosc pears (about 1 pound)
2 tablespoons butter
Salt and freshly ground pepper

Peel the celery roots and cut them into 1-inch cubes. Boil in lightly salted water until tender when pierced, about 15 minutes. Lift them from the water and drain in a colander. Add the lemon juice to the water in the pan and return to heat. Peel, quarter, and core the pears. Add them to the water and simmer for about 15 minutes, or until tender when pierced. Drain the pears well, then puree in a food processor or through a food mill with the celery root. Beat in the butter and salt and pepper to taste. Reheat in an double boiler before serving, if necessary. Makes about 3½ cups, serving 4 or 5.

# Turnip-Apple Gratin

*One of my favorite flavor themes is the interplay of earthy and sweet flavors, which is exactly what happens among the turnips, potatoes, and apples. They can be cooked and mashed together hours in advance and reheated at dinnertime.*

Peel and slice turnips and potatoes. Peel, core, and slice the apple. Combine in a large saucepan, cover with water, and boil until all are tender—15 to 20 minutes. Drain and mash (or process) with the milk and butter. Add salt and pepper to taste.

Transfer to a 6-cup soufflé dish (or casserole). Sprinkle the top with cheese. Heat in a 400° F. oven until the cheese bubbles and browns slightly. Serve hot. Makes 6 servings.

1 pound turnips (2 or 3 medium)
1 pound potatoes (3 or 4 medium)
1 large apple
½ cup milk
2 tablespoons butter
Salt and freshly ground pepper
1 cup (4 ounces) grated Swiss cheese

# Winter Gratin

*The flavors of winter in this side dish are based on a dish served to me by the late and wonderful chef, Josephine Araldo.*

¾ pound mushrooms
¾ pound Belgian endive (3 or 4 small heads)
1 bunch leeks
2 tablespoons butter
2 tablespoons oil
½ cup chicken stock
Salt and freshly ground pepper
½ cup ground walnuts

Slice the mushrooms ⅛- to ¼-inch thick. Cut the bottoms off the endive, and cut it crosswise into ½-inch pieces. The leaves will separate. Cut the leeks off 1½ to 2 inches into the green portion. Clean the leeks and cut them in half lengthwise. Cut off the bottoms and cut them crosswise into ¼-inch slices.

In a large, deep skillet or sauté pan, melt the butter and oil and sauté the leeks and mushrooms until the leeks begin to soften. Add the stock and the endive, cover the pan, and simmer for 10 minutes. When all the vegetables are soft, drain them well, reserving the stock, and transfer them to a gratin pan or another baking pan.

If you used unsalted stock, boil it down to 3 or 4 tablespoons and use it to moisten the vegetables. If the stock is salted, use 3 or 4 tablespoons of it without reducing it. Sprinkle the walnuts on top. This much can be done in advance. Before serving, heat the vegetables in a 425° F. oven until heated through and the walnuts are crisp. Makes 6 servings.

# Oven Parmesan Chips

*Serve this flavorful alternative to potato chips right out of the oven as an appetizer or side dish with an informal meal.*

Preheat oven to 425° F. Cut washed, unpeeled potatoes into ⅛-inch thick round slices, and place in a single layer on lightly buttered baking sheets.

Melt butter in a small saucepan and add onion, salt and pepper to taste, and paprika. Brush just enough of the butter mixture on the potatoes to make them glisten, and bake for 15 to 20 minutes, or until the potatoes are crisp and golden. Sprinkle with Parmesan. Makes 4 to 6 servings.

4 medium potatoes (about ⅓ pound each)
4 tablespoons (¼ cup) butter
1 tablespoon grated onion
Salt and freshly ground pepper to taste
Dash paprika
2 tablespoons grated Parmesan

# Potato Pancakes
# (Latkes)

*Traditional at Hanukkah in Jewish households, but delicious any time of the year, these pancakes are not side dishes, at least not in our family. The* latkes *are the center of attention, cooked fresh and served around the kitchen table with sour cream, apple sauce and cinnamon mixed with sugar.*

1 pound peeled baking potatoes
¼ cup grated onion
1 teaspoon salt
¼ teaspoon freshly ground pepper
2 eggs, lightly beaten
2 to 4 tablespoons matzoh meal or cracker meal
Oil for pan frying

Grate the potatoes into a large bowl. Immediately stir in the onion, salt, and enough matzoh meal or cracker meal to make a thick batter. (If the grated potatoes are allowed to stand exposed to air before mixing with the remaining ingredients, they turn brown; not a disaster, but not as attractive.)

Put enough oil in a large frying pan or griddle to film the surface generously. Heat the pan over a moderate flame. When the oil is hot, spoon about ¼ cup of the potato batter into the pan for each pancake. Allow a half inch of space between pancakes. Regulate the heat so that the surface of the pancakes browns and crisps in about 5 minutes on each side. With a spatula, turn the pancakes to brown on the other side. Serve them immediately with small bowls of sour cream, apple sauce, and cinnamon and sugar. Makes about 12 pancakes, enough for 3 or 4 normal appetites.

# Sweet Potato Pancakes

*These golden, naturally sweet pancakes are made from sweet potatoes,
not sweetened white potatoes. They are especially good for breakfast with
sausages, apple sauce, and maple syrup, or for dinner to accompany roast
meats or poultry.*

Peel and grate the sweet potato. In a bowl, beat together all the
ingredients except the oil. Set a large skillet over moderate heat and film the
bottom with 2 tablespoons of oil, shortening or drippings. Place quarter-cup
blobs of the potato mixture in the hot fat, and press them down with the back of
a spatula to form more-or-less round cakes about 4 inches wide. Do not crowd
the skillet; do this in batches if necessary. Cook about 5 minutes on each side,
until well browned, adding more fat to the skillet if necessary. Makes 8 pancakes.

1 large sweet potato (about 1 pound)
⅓ cup whipping cream
1 egg
2 tablespoons flour
1 teaspoon salt
½ teaspoon freshly ground pepper
¼ cup vegetable oil, shortening or
  bacon drippings

# Carrot and Turnip Pancakes

*Vegetable pancakes can be made with more than just potatoes—and they are versatile and good with just about any meat or poultry. These hearty pancakes are also good served with scrambled eggs or bacon for an informal supper or brunch.*

3 large carrots (about ½ pound)
2 turnips (about ½ pound)
2 eggs
2 tablespoons flour
2 tablespoons chopped parsley
½ teaspoon dried leaf thyme
½ teaspoon salt
¼ teaspoon freshly ground pepper
Olive oil, shortening, vegetable
  oil, or bacon drippings for frying

Peel the carrots and turnips, then shred them on the large holes of a grater or use the shredding disk of a food processor. Pick up the shredded vegetables a fistful at a time and squeeze as much moisture as you can from them. (The juice makes a pleasant drink.) Drop the vegetables into a bowl and add the remaining ingredients except the oil. Beat well until completely mixed.

Place a large skillet over moderate heat and film the bottom with oil, shortening, or drippings. When the oil is quite hot, shape quarter-cup blobs of the carrot-turnip mixture into roundish cakes about 3 inches across. Fry 2 to 3 minutes on each side, until well browned. Fry the remaining pancakes the same way, adding more fat to the pan as necessary. Keep them warm in a low oven until all are cooked and you're ready to serve them. Makes about 10 pancakes.

# Cheese Pot

*This tangy cheese spread bears no resemblance to the packaged cheese spreads sold in grocery stores. Flavor it as you like with crumbled bacon, diced roasted peppers, or chopped fresh herbs. It's great for spreading on crackers, and if reheated gently in a double boiler, it makes a dandy cheese sauce for vegetables.*

Melt the butter in a heavy saucepan over medium heat. Add the cheese and stir for a minute, until melted. Add the egg yolks and half-and-half and whisk until smooth. Remove from heat and season with salt and pepper, then add several drops of Tabasco for a spicy spread. Pour into a small decorative bowl or crock and press a piece of plastic wrap directly on the surface (to keep a skin from forming). Chill for several hours, until firm. If you wish to flavor the cheese as suggested, chill it for an hour or so—just until it begins to hold its shape—then stir in the flavoring and chill until firm. Makes about 1½ cups.

2 tablespoons butter
½ pound sharp Cheddar, grated
2 egg yolks
½ cup half-and-half
Salt and freshly ground pepper
Tabasco

# Yogurt Cheese

*Loni Kuhn, a noted San Francisco cooking teacher and sometime substitute host on the "KCBS Kitchen," shared this with me and the listeners on a program devoted to low-fat, healthy cooking. Look for a yogurt that contains no gelatin, agar, or pectin. Usually, only small, local brands fit the bill. In the San Francisco Bay Area, these include Pavel, Nancy's, and Natural and Kosher.*

**1 quart nonfat yogurt**

Line a sieve with a dish towel or double thickness of cheesecloth. Place the sieve on a bowl deep enough so the whey will not touch the bottom of the sieve. Pour the yogurt into the sieve and cover with the ends of the towel. Refrigerate for 18 to 24 hours. The cheese will then be very thick. One quart of yogurt when drained well yields about 1¼ cups cheese.

Yogurt cheese is versatile and can, depending on flavoring, substitute handsomely for mayonnaise or herb cheese (spread on fresh pears, for example). This yogurt cheese has no fat or cholesterol and only about 13 calories per tablespoon.

*Some seasoning and serving ideas:* Mix with a little kirsch or other fruit liqueur and a bit of sugar, if desired, and serve with fresh berries.

Mix with a bit of honey and serve with fresh pears for dessert.

Put in a food processor with sun-dried tomatoes, roasted red peppers, and garlic; spread on *crostini* (Italian bread toast) or baguettes.

Stir into hot pasta.

Put in a food processor with fresh thyme, tarragon, and garlic to make a fine dip or spread, or combine with chopped fresh green chili, cilantro, garlic, and cumin to dip with jicama.

Serve at breakfast on toast with or without jam.

Thin it with a bit of milk or chicken broth and use it instead of béchamel to layer in lasagne or moussaka.

**Q.** *Do you have a recipe for San Francisco sourdough starter for my son in Washington, D.C.?*

**A.** I can give you a recipe, but the tricky part is to get the starter going. Unfortunately, I know of no one who sells a true sourdough starter. Those commercial sourdough starter kits are nothing more than regular yeast, flour, and flavoring.

There is a myth surrounding San Francisco sourdough bread, that it cannot be made anywhere else. There is supposedly something in the Bay Area's atmosphere. Sounds romantic, but it's not true. True San Francisco sourdough bread is the result of the interaction of two organisms. One is a yeast that is different from ordinary bread yeast in that it ferments slowly and tolerates much more acetic acid—vinegar—than ordinary bread yeast. The other is a bacterium, actually called *Lactobacillus sanfrancisco*, that works on the dough to create a lot of acetic acid while the bread rises. These two organisms work together to make the characteristic sour flavor and dense texture from slow rising.

You may not be able to make a true sourdough bread, but you can get pretty close by making a starter of **2 cups each yogurt and flour** mixed with **1 package of active dry yeast** dissolved in ½ **cup warm water** with **1 teaspoon sugar**. Allow the mixture to stand, covered, at cool room temperature for 2 to 3 days, then proceed to make bread dough from half the starter plus 4 cups flour, 1 tablespoon salt and 1½ cups water to make a dough.

# CHAPTER FIVE:

# ROBUST DISHES

# ROBUST DISHES

The popularity of salads, egg dishes, and beans as focal points of a meal seems particularly prominent in California. Perhaps it is the mild climate, which lends itself to less elaborate meals. Perhaps it is the high level of health consciousness that leads Californians to prefer alternatives to a steady diet of meat and potatoes. Whatever the reasons, I notice that my radio recipe collection actually contains more main dish salads than beef dishes.

What makes a good main dish salad? Other than compatible flavors, the combination of fresh produce with meat, fish, or poultry should offer contrasts in color and texture. Being a salad, it should be edible with just a fork, although I am of the school that advocates occasionally using a piece of bread to help the bits of salad onto the fork. I like dressings for these salads to be shy on vinegar to make them more compatible with wine. To make the best companions with these salads, lighter wines of any color should be generous in fruit aromas and flavors.

Although Europeans eat eggs mostly at lunch and dinner, we tend to relegate them to breakfast. Like most people, I am content to serve eggs scrambled, fried, poached, or cooked into omelets, which is probably why the selection of egg recipes included here is slim. To make up for it, here are my foolproof techniques for two ways to cook eggs that seem to fluster many people:

*Hard-Cooked Eggs:* I don't think of them as hard-boiled because they should not boil for more than a few seconds. Put the eggs in a saucepan and cover them with *cold* water. Put the water over a high flame, and as it reaches a boil, cover the pan and take it off the burner. Let it stand 15 minutes, during which time the eggs cook perfectly. They will not overcook because the water is constantly cooling.

Hard-cooked eggs will peel best if you remove the shells while they are still warm. Pour off the water and roll the eggs around in the pan to crack them. As soon as they are cool enough to handle, peel them. Keep them refrigerated if they are not eaten within an hour or two.

*Omelets:*  For home use, I recommend a nonstick omelet pan, 6 or 7 inches in diameter. Larger pans make flat omelets. The classic omelet pan is uncoated steel, but the first omelet or two always sticks in those pans. A restaurant chef who is going to make 50 or 100 omelets doesn't care if the first one is wasted. At home, I prefer to make every omelet count.

Break two or three eggs into a small bowl. Do not add water or milk. Blend the yolk and white with a fork made of plastic or wood. (It will be used later to stir the eggs in the pan, and metal would mar the nonstick surface.) Heat the pan for a minute or two over a high-moderate heat. Melt a teaspoon or two of butter in the pan (or use clarified butter). Pour in the eggs and start stirring them with the fork, as if you are making scrambled eggs. As they solidify, pat them into a circular shape and sprinkle them lightly with salt and pepper. Add a filling, if you like, and turn the omelet out onto a heated plate.

My technique for turning out an omelet is to grasp the handle of the pan from underneath, scoot the edge of the omelet out of the pan onto the plate, then invert the pan over the plate so the omelet turns over on itself.

The egg dishes in this chapter are basically breakfast fare, but I also like to serve them for light lunches or late suppers, especially the Garlicky Poached Eggs (page 221) and Frittata Monte Vertine (page 222).

Bean dishes, long out of favor, are beginning to come back into vogue, especially when the beans are combined with vegetables for side dishes. With a loaf of bread or bowl of rice, any of these bean dishes makes a fine stick-to-your-ribs main course.

# Fish Citrus Salad

*This started out as a way to use up cooked fish, but it became so popular around our house that we rewrote the recipe to start with freshly cooked fish. The interplay of flavors calls for a lightly sweet white wine such as a fresh, young Gewürztraminer.*

Cut the fish fillets into ¾-inch cubes. Poach the fish in a saucepan with enough wine to barely cover the fish and onion rings for 8 minutes. Let them cool in the liquid, then strain and discard the liquid.

Peel the oranges and slice them thin crosswise. Remove the seeds. For grapefruit, peel and section, then cut the sections in two or three pieces. Remove the seeds. Peel the avocados and cut them into cubes. Toss the cubes in a bit of the grapefruit juice to keep them from browning.

Make the dressing by blending the oil, juice, and mustard. Season with salt and pepper to taste.

To serve the salad family style, toss the ingredients with the dressing and serve. As a fancier presentation, line the bottom of the salad plate with overlapping slices of orange, surround with avocado cubes, and pile the fish cubes in the center. Drape the onions over the fish cubes and drizzle the salad dressing on top. Makes 4 servings.

1 pound large fish fillets (salmon, halibut, shark)
1 to 2 cups dry white wine
1 large onion, sliced and separated into rings
3 or 4 medium oranges or 2 grapefruit
2 medium avocados
⅓ cup olive oil
¼ cup grapefruit juice
1 teaspoon Dijon mustard
Salt and freshly ground pepper

# Cantaloupe Stuffed with Shrimp

*This is one of my favorite ways to present a simple seafood salad. It is especially refreshing on a warm day. A good dressing for this is C.K.'s Salad Dressing (page 175).*

For each serving:
½ medium to large cantaloupe
⅓ pound bay shrimp
1 ounce crabmeat (optional)
½ medium tomato
2 tablespoons finely chopped sweet onion or green onion
2 to 4 tablespoons creamy salad dressing

Cut the cantaloupe in half. (It's pretty to do it with a zigzag cut.) Scoop out the seeds. Scoop out and reserve a little of the melon, too, to make a bigger cavity. Peel, seed, and chop the tomato.

In a bowl, place the shrimp, optional crabmeat, tomato, and chopped onion. Toss them together with enough dressing to just moisten the ingredients. Spoon the salad into the cavity of the cantaloupe halves.

Chop the melon that you scooped out to widen the cavity. Mix it with some of the remaining dressing and spoon it over the salad just before serving it. Serve this with crusty French bread.

# Chicken-Melon Salad

*Moist cubes of poached chicken breast combined with pieces of sweet, ripe melon make a refreshing and colorful salad. It's also a good way to extend a small amount of chicken to serve several people.*

Toss together the chicken, melon, lemon juice, parsley, and cilantro. Season lightly with salt and pepper and toss again. Blend in the mayonnaise and chill thoroughly before serving. Taste and season with additional salt and pepper if necessary. Serve the salad on a bed of crisp, shredded iceberg lettuce. Makes 3 or 4 servings.

2 cups diced, cooked chicken
2 cups melon balls or cubes (honey-dew, Cranshaw, and orange honey-dew are especially good)
1 tablespoon lemon juice
¼ cup chopped parsley
1 tablespoon chopped cilantro
Salt and freshly ground pepper
½ cup mayonnaise, preferably home-made (page 295)
½ head iceberg lettuce, shredded

# Chicken Salad with Mango Mayonnaise

*Mango is the richest, most flavorful fruit I know, and its ripe pungency and the smooth texture of its puree transforms a simple mayonnaise into a celestial salad dressing for chicken or fish. To find a ripe mango, look for ones with no green streaks that have an intense aroma and feel a bit soft when squeezed gently in the palm of the hand.*

2 whole chicken breasts
1 ripe mango
1 egg yolk
½ teaspoon salt
¼ teaspoon freshly ground pepper
2 tablespoons lemon juice or white
    wine vinegar
½ cup olive oil
½ head iceberg lettuce, shredded
1 grapefruit, sectioned (optional)
2 tablespoons chopped parsley

Poach the chicken breasts in simmering salted water to cover for about 10 minutes, or use the Chicken Steeping Method (page 72), then set aside and let them cool to room temperature in the liquid. Remove the cooled meat from the bones and cut it into long strips about ½-inch wide. (The salad will be better if the chicken is never chilled after cooking, but if you aren't serving it within an hour or two, you will have to chill it. Let it come to room temperature before assembling the salad.)

Peel the mango and cut the flesh from the fibrous pit; drop the pulp into a food processor. Add the egg yolk, salt, and pepper and process until smooth. Add the lemon juice or vinegar, and with the machine running, pour in the oil in a thin stream; you will have a smooth, creamy sauce.

Spread the shredded lettuce out on a large platter. Arrange the chicken strips over the lettuce. You can, if you wish, intersperse grapefruit sections among the chicken. Spoon the dressing over all. Sprinkle with parsley and serve within an hour. Makes 4 servings.

# Roasted Onion and Salame Salad

*Roasted onions lose their sharp bite and become quite sweet and mild. Combined with the olives and salame, this makes a wonderful luncheon salad or antipasto.*

Preheat the oven to 350° F.

Place the onions on a rack set in a baking pan and roast in the oven for about 1 hour 15 minutes, until tender when pierced. Let stand until cooled to room temperature.

Peel the onions; with a very sharp knife, cut them into ½-inch thick slices, separating the rings as you work. Arrange the lettuce leaves around the perimeter of a large platter and mound the onions in the middle. Lay the salame slices around the onions and sprinkle the olives over all. In a tightly capped jar, shake together the oil, vinegar, mustard, garlic, and pepper to taste. Pour over the salad and serve. Makes 6 servings.

6 yellow onions, unpeeled
12 or more leaves romaine or butter lettuce
6 ounces salame, thinly sliced (1½ cups)
½ cup oil-cured olives, pitted
⅓ cup olive oil
2 tablespoons red wine vinegar
1 teaspoon dry mustard
1 clove garlic, minced
Freshly ground pepper

# Roast Pork and Papaya Salad

*Leftover roast pork makes a splendid comeback in this colorful salad, which makes a fine luncheon dish. It combines many tastes and textures: the crunchy green onion, peppery watercress, hearty pork, and soft, sweet papaya all tossed in a sesame vinaigrette. Use Chinese roast pork, if available, for a unique flavor combination.*

1½ to 2 cups roast pork
1 large papaya
1 bunch green onions, thinly sliced
   (about 1 cup)
1 bunch watercress, large stems
   removed
¼ cup olive oil
1 tablespoon Oriental sesame oil
1½ tablespoons wine vinegar
Salt and freshly ground pepper

Cut the pork in bite-size strips. Peel the papaya, remove seeds, and cut into strips the same size as the pork. In a bowl, toss together the pork, papaya, green onions, and watercress; set aside.

In a small, screw-topped jar, place the olive and sesame oils, vinegar, and salt and pepper to taste. Cap tightly and shake vigorously. Pour over the salad and toss well. Serve at room temperature, with lots of warm crusty bread. Makes 4 servings.

# Turkey-Chutney Salad

*After the roast turkey, the age-old question is what to do with the leftovers besides sandwiches. This is one of my favorite answers. You may even find yourself cooking turkey just to make this salad.*

Toss all the ingredients together and serve them on lettuce or stuffed into half an avocado, cantaloupe, or papaya. Makes 4 servings.

2 ½ cups diced cooked turkey
½ cup chutney
2 green onions, thinly sliced
2 tablespoons chopped parsley
½ cup toasted walnut pieces
¼ cup mayonnaise

# François' Scramble

*François Metraux is a Swiss friend and a chef who learned his craft at the Hotel School in Lausanne. We used to meet for early morning handball games, after which he would cook us breakfast: this. It still hits the spot.*

2 tomatoes
½ onion or 1 shallot
2 teaspoons butter
1 tablespoon cream cheese (optional)
4 eggs
Salt and freshly ground pepper

Peel, seed, and roughly chop the tomatoes. Chop the onion or shallot. Sauté the onions or shallots and the tomatoes in the butter until the tomatoes are dry, about 6 minutes. Crumble or pinch the cream cheese into the mixture. Beat the eggs with a fork as for scrambled eggs and add them to the pan. Cook the mixture, stirring it occasionally, until the eggs are set, about 2 minutes. Season to taste with salt and pepper.

This is delicious by itself or with leftover meat or vegetables stirred into the mixture to heat through before adding the egg. It makes a nice supper with fresh steamed or boiled vegetables and crusty bread for a texture contrast. Makes 2 servings.

*Note:* The tomato mixture, which in fancy French circles is called *tomates fondues*, can be made in quantity and kept refrigerated for several days.

# Garlicky Poached Eggs

*Eggs seem to take longer to poach in liquids other than water, so give these a few seconds longer than you normally would. This makes a nice light supper dish.*

Separate the garlic into cloves and wallop them several times with the side of a knife or cleaver to loosen the papery skin, but don't worry about removing it entirely. In a skillet or saucepan about 7 or 8 inches in diameter, bring the smashed garlic to a boil with the stock and wine. Reduce the heat, cover, and simmer gently for about 30 minutes, until garlic is soft. Remove the garlic with a slotted spoon and press it through a strainer or sieve to extract the buttery flesh, leaving the skins behind. Reserve the buttery flesh.

Crack the eggs into the simmering liquid, dropping each in a different spot, and poach gently for about 6 minutes, until set. With a skimmer or slotted spoon, transfer the eggs to paper towels to drain. They may now wait for 30 minutes or so.

Skim the poaching liquid to remove any stray bits of egg that broke off, then over highest heat, rapidly reduce to about ¾ cup.

When ready to serve, place each egg on a piece of toast, and set in a preheated 350° F. oven for 6 minutes. Then over medium heat swirl the butter and cream into the liquid, and whisk in the dissolved cornstarch and the reserved garlic. Place the eggs on plates and spoon the sauce over them. Makes 2 to 4 servings.

1 head garlic
2 cups chicken stock (homemade or low-salt canned broth)
1 cup dry white wine
4 eggs
4 slices lightly toasted bread
4 tablespoons (½ stick) soft butter
¼ cup cream
1 teaspoon cornstarch mixed with 1 tablespoon water

# Frittata Monte Vertine

*At the Monte Vertine estate near Radda in Chianti, the cook served a series of three wonderful frittatas as first courses. One was especially delicious and fascinating. It looked like it was made from mustard greens, but it tasted sweet, like onions. It turns out that red onions react with eggs to turn green, hence the misleading color. Maybe that's where Dr. Seuss got his green eggs and ham . . .*

1 large red onion
3 tablespoons extra virgin olive oil
1 dozen fresh basil leaves
2 tablespoons Italian parsley leaves
8 eggs
Salt and freshly ground pepper

Peel the onion, cut it in half lengthwise, then into slices about ⅛-inch thick. Preheat the broiler.

In a large skillet (10 or 12 inches across), sauté the onions over gentle heat in the olive oil. When they are soft, about 10 to 15 minutes, stir in the basil and parsley. Raise the heat to medium and add the eggs. Cook the eggs, stirring gently, until they are set. Season lightly with salt and pepper. Slide the pan under the broiler to set the eggs, then invert the frittata onto a serving plate so the browned side is up. Makes 6 to 8 appetizer servings.

# Breakfast Burritos

*Anyone who likes* huevos rancheros *ought to give this a try. The flavors are similar, but this is more convenient to eat.*

**M**elt the butter in a skillet, add the eggs, season with salt and pepper, and cook slowly until softly set. Meanwhile, heat the tortillas in a regular or microwave oven. Sprinkle 2 or 3 tablespoons of cheese on each tortilla. Open the chilies so they lay flat, and place one down the middle of each tortilla. Spoon the scrambled eggs over the chilies, and top with a spoonful of salsa. Roll each tortilla up like a burrito and serve. Makes 6 servings.

**4 tablespoons (½ stick) butter**
**12 eggs, lightly beaten**
**Salt and freshly ground pepper**
**6 large flour tortillas**
**6 mild whole green chilies (about one 7-ounce can), seeded**
**1 cup (4 ounces) grated Cheddar or Monterey Jack**
**Salsa**

**Q.** *What are these low-cholesterol eggs I have been seeing?*

**A.** Sorry, early reports of low-cholesterol eggs were exaggerated. All eggs are about 15 percent lower in cholesterol than the official nutrition books say. The reason is that laying chickens were fed differently when tests to determine the cholesterol were done years ago. The promoters of the "low-cholesterol" eggs compared their eggs with the listings in the standard reference work, *Nutritive Values of Foods*, published by the U.S. Department of Agriculture. The figures are being revised for the next edition.

# Bacon and Egg Breakfast "Pie"

*A one-skillet breakfast dish, with a "crust" of sautéed potatoes, topped with bacon and a creamy egg custard. You can fry the bacon and boil and dice the potatoes the night before, then do the final assembly and cooking just before serving. Serve with buttered toast and preserves.*

8 slices (about ½ pound) bacon
4 large boiling potatoes (about 1½ pounds)
3 tablespoons bacon drippings or butter
1 onion, finely chopped
Salt and freshly ground pepper
8 eggs
½ cup milk

Fry the bacon until crisp. Drain on paper towels and crumble. Discard all but 3 tablespoons of the bacon fat. Boil the potatoes and dice them.

Heat the bacon fat (or use butter) in a 10-inch skillet (preferably cast iron) over moderate heat. Add the onion and cook for about 10 minutes, stirring occasionally, until lightly browned. Add the diced potatoes and cook for about 10 minutes more, stirring and tossing frequently, until potatoes are partially browned. Season with salt and pepper. Sprinkle potatoes with the crumbled bacon and turn heat to low.

Preheat the oven to 400° F.

Beat the eggs and milk together and season with salt and pepper to taste. Pour over the bacon and potatoes, cover the skillet (with a makeshift foil cover if necessary) and cook over low heat for 5 minutes. Uncover the pan and put in the oven for 5 to 10 minutes longer, or just until set. Cut into wedges to serve. Makes 4 to 6 servings.

# Dutch Baby

*Al Hart, my co-host on the "KCBS Kitchen," makes this for breakfast two or three times a week. It is actually easier than making pancakes, and looks spectacular.*

Put the butter in a 10-inch skillet and place in a 425° F. oven to melt and get the skillet very hot.

Meanwhile, put the eggs in a blender or food processor. Blend them for 1 minute, or until they are very light and fluffy, then add the milk and let it blend for 30 seconds. With the motor running, pour in the flour a little at a time, letting it blend until the batter is very smooth. Add the pinch of salt and stop the blender.

When the pan and the butter are very hot, remove them from the oven and pour in the batter. Immediately return the pan to the oven and let it bake for 20 minutes. It should puff up, then collapse in the center while it browns appetizingly.

Serve the Dutch Baby hot with a pat or two of butter, a generous sprinkling of powdered sugar, and a squeeze or two of lemon. Or fill it with fresh fruit. Eat it while it's hot. Makes 2 servings.

**5⅓ tablespoons (⅔ stick) butter**
**3 eggs**
**⅔ cup milk**
**⅔ cup flour**
**Pinch of salt**

# White Beans and Fennel

*This hearty combination can either be an accompaniment to roast meats or a main course, if you toss in some leftover diced ham, roast beef, or pork before baking.*

1½ pounds fennel (about 3 bulbs)
2 tablespoons butter
1 onion, thinly sliced
Salt and freshly ground pepper
2 15-ounce cans white beans, drained and rinsed or 4 cups cooked white beans
1 teaspoon dried basil
4 slices bacon

Preheat the oven to 375° F.

Trim the feathery tops off the fennel, and cut the bulb part into ½-inch slices. Melt the butter in a large skillet over moderate heat, then add the fennel and onion. Cook gently, stirring frequently, for about 30 minutes, until the vegetables are softened and wilted but not browned; they will actually steam in some of their own juices. Season with salt and pepper to taste.

Toss the beans and basil together in a large bowl, then add the onions and fennel and toss again to mix. Place in a 1½-quart baking dish, top with the bacon, and bake covered for 30 minutes. Remove the cover and bake for another 30 minutes. Makes 6 servings.

# Slow Beans

*Serve these beans with all kinds of roast meat and poultry or as a main dish with rice and a green salad. It can cook for hours in the oven right along with the roasting meat, and you can stop the cooking at any point and continue later. Total cooking time is 4 hours.*

In a casserole of about 3-quart capacity, place half of the beans. Peel and thinly slice the tomatoes, top the beans with half the tomato slices, and spread this with half of the onions. Repeat the layers. Bake in a 300° to 350° F. oven for about 2 hours, stirring once or twice, until the tomatoes and onions have softened and given off their juices.

Meanwhile, cut the bacon into 1-inch pieces and blanch for 3 minutes in boiling water. Top the beans with half of the bacon and return to the oven for about an hour, or until the bacon is cooked and lightly browned. Poke the bacon down into the beans and vegetables, stir in the tomato sauce, then top with the remaining bacon. Return to the oven and bake about an hour or so more, until the bacon is lightly browned. Serve now, or keep warm in the oven (with the heat turned off) until you are ready. Makes 6 servings.

**4 cups cooked kidney beans**
**4 medium to large tomatoes**
**2 onions, finely chopped**
**8 slices bacon (about ½ pound)**
**½ cup tomato sauce**

Q. *Is there a way to de-gas beans?*

A. Not completely, but scientists have identified the chemical culprit in beans that causes flatulence. They haven't bred it out of the beans yet, although they are trying, but they did find that this chemical is heat sensitive and water soluble. The method is to start the beans in plenty of cold water, bring them to a boil, and let them stand for 5 to 10 minutes. Drain them well and repeat the process three times. Then let them cook normally.

# Eggplant and Bean Stew

*Fresh cranberry beans are only in season a short time, in early autumn, but there is nothing like them. This dish is great with roast lamb or chicken.*

1 pound eggplant (Japanese if
    possible)
1 pound fresh cranberry beans
2 tablespoons olive oil
Salt and freshly ground pepper
1 teaspoon dried Provençal herbs
    (thyme, rosemary, chervil)
1 cup marinara sauce

Slice eggplant ½-inch thick. (Slice on a slant if using Japanese eggplant.) Sprinkle with salt and set aside to drain.

Shell the beans. Cover them with water in a saucepan, and boil until tender, about 15 minutes. Add more water if necessary.

Wipe the eggplant dry. In a large skillet, sauté the eggplant in the olive oil to brown it. Season with salt and plenty of pepper and Provençal herbs. When the eggplant is browned, add marinara sauce and the beans, with some of the water they were cooked in. Simmer until the eggplant is done—about 5 minutes. If the mixture is dry, add more of the bean water. Makes 6 to 8 servings.

# White Bean and Lentil Puree

*This irresistible mixture is a wonderful dip for tortilla chips, but is not so pungent and garlicky that it can't be used as a filling for omelets, or to accompany roast lamb.*

Combine the beans, lentils, and garlic in a food processor and whirl until smooth. With the machine running, pour in the oil. Season to taste with salt and pepper. If serving as a dip, stir in the parsley now. If you are serving it hot, as a vegetable or filling, reheat the mixture slowly in a pan or in a double boiler, and add the parsley just before serving. Makes 4 servings.

1½ cups cooked white beans
1½ cups cooked lentils
2 large cloves garlic
¼ cup olive oil
Salt and freshly ground pepper
2 tablespoons chopped parsley

Q. *I have been cooking pinto beans for four hours and they just won't get soft. What happened?*

A. I'll bet you added onions and perhaps tomatoes to the beans for flavor. You have to wait until the beans are soft before adding anything containing acid, like onions and tomatoes, because the acidity interferes with the cooking process. Flavor the beans with a meat bone or herbs if you like, but no acidity until they are soft.

# CHAPTER SIX:

# SWEETS

# SWEETS

When dessert rolls around—and in some of the finest restaurants a selection of temptations arrayed on a fancy serving cart literally does—the items that lure me fastest are the simplest and homiest. Give me an apple crisp over Gâteau St. Honoré any day. The compilation of cakes, cookies, ice creams, and other sweets in this chapter reflects this point of view. Given the listeners' enthusiastic response to these desserts, I think I have plenty of company. For all the emphasis on healthy eating these days, everyone, it seems, still has a raging sweet tooth.

I feel obliged to call your attention to several items in particular, because they are among the most popular recipes I have ever offered. Every time I mention them on the "KCBS Kitchen," I receive a mountain of requests.

I had never run across anything quite like the Blueberry "Pudding" (page 244) until a listener sent it to me. An inverted custard cup draws in the excess moisture as the berries cook under a layer of cake batter, yielding a unique and wonderful texture in the berries. Two unique ice creams are the Bittersweet Chocolate Flake Ice Cream (page 253), which makes its own fragile chocolate chips as it is mixed, and the Cheesecake Ice Cream (page 256), which tastes like frozen cheesecake because of its secret ingredient, buttermilk. The Peanut Butter Pie (page 271) hides its peanut layers on either side of a custard filling, separating it from the crust on the bottom and the meringue on top. As a devoted fan of cookies that crunch, I am delighted at the positive response the Crisp Oatmeal Cookies (page 283) always trigger. They are thin and audible. Secret Toffee (page 288) is one of those hard-to-believe recipes that becomes addictive because something so simple can turn out so good. As a friend told me, "That stuff is dangerous. It's too easy to make."

For those who love madeleines, I urge you to try baking my

Proust's Madeleines (page 280). Although the recipe is a bit more complicated than most, it was arrived at after long and frustrating experience with other, simpler recipes, none of which quite captured the delicate velvety texture of the best madeleines, which tug at your heart as well as your palate. Normally, my instincts are to simplify every task as much as possible, but I can't quite duplicate that texture when I shorten the procedure.

Let me interject a final word about dessert wines. Although wine snobs often sniff in derision at sweet wines, real connoisseurs know that some of the most glorious wines in the world are sweet. A great vintage Port, a 15- to 20-year-old Sauternes, or a late-harvest Riesling are so rich and complex in flavor that they can and sometimes should be consumed without accompanying food. In truth, with great dessert wines, the best foods to serve are simple cookies or pound cakes.

Certain sweet wines, however, are especially good with desserts—Moscato d'Asti from Italy, sweet Champagnes from France (often labeled, paradoxically, "semi-dry"), and medium-sweet Rieslings (labeled "late harvest" or "*auslese*") from California or Germany. The most important trick in matching desserts and wines is to make the dessert less sweet than the wine. I have also found that fruit desserts and non-chocolate cakes and cookies are the most wine-friendly. In particular, try the Light Honey Mousse (page 238), Blueberry Tart (page 266), Fresh Pear Upside-Down Cake (page 275), and Buckwheat Cardamom Shortbread (page 284).

# Banana Crème Brulée

*Bananas, caramel, and custard are a sublime combination. The thin, candied layer of sugar on top, often unpredictable and difficult to make under the broiler, is made here in just a few seconds, with the bottom of a super-hot iron skillet. Traditionally,* crème brulée *is fired under a salamander—a thick, small, round piece of iron with a long handle to be heated on a burner then set directly over the sugar-topped custard in a ramekin, thus caramelizing it in seconds. I thought a hot skillet would work just as well, and it did.*

1 large or 2 small bananas
4 egg yolks
2 whole eggs
⅓ cup granulated sugar
2 cups milk, heated
1 teaspoon vanilla
½ cup brown sugar

Preheat the oven to 325° F.

Cut the banana into ½-inch thick slices, spreading them evenly over the bottom of a 9-inch pie plate.

Whisk the egg yolks and eggs together in a heavy-bottomed saucepan, and then whisk in the sugar. Add the milk and blend thoroughly. Set over medium heat and whisk constantly for about 5 minutes, until the custard thickens slightly and you see definite wisps of steam rising—don't let it boil, or it will curdle. Add the vanilla and pour into the pie pan over the bananas. Set the pie pan in a large pan and add hot water to come halfway up the pie pan. Bake for 20 minutes, remove from the water, and set the pie pan in the refrigerator for several hours or overnight.

When the custard is thoroughly chilled, dump the brown sugar into a strainer. With your fingers or a spoon, force it through the strainer onto the top of the custard, forming as even a layer as you can. Smooth the sugar, pressing it down gently, with the back of a spoon.

Heat a small iron skillet over highest heat until the bottom of the skillet is almost hazy white—as though you were making some "blackened" dish. On a gas stove, this takes about 5 to 7 minutes. With 2 pot holders, pick up the skillet by the handle and hold it directly on top of the brown sugar—if the skillet is hot enough, the sugar will sizzle and caramelize almost instantly; if it's not hot enough, the sugar sticks to the skillet. Move the skillet around slowly if necessary to cover the entire area, then lift it off and set aside in a safe place; it's still hot!

Let the custard sit for about 10 minutes so the sugar can harden into a thin sheet, and serve. (If your first attempt didn't work, and the sugar sticks to the pan, simply sieve another thin layer of sugar over the custard, wipe off the skillet, reheat it, and try again.) Makes 6 servings.

# Coffee Mousse

*Il Sole restaurant on Lake Maggiore, in northern Italy, is the source of this simple dessert with extraordinary flavor. To make the coffee very strong, use enough ground coffee to make 1 cup but drip through only ⅓ to ½ cup hot water, which is just enough to make ¼ cup; some of the water is needed to moisten the grounds.*

6 egg yolks
6 tablespoons sugar
3 egg whites
1 cup whipping cream
¼ cup very strong coffee
1 teaspoon instant coffee

In a bowl, whisk the egg yolks with half of the sugar until very smooth. In a clean bowl with clean beaters, whip the egg whites until they form soft peaks. Whip in the remaining sugar. Whip the cream in another bowl, then fold it into the egg yolks along with the coffee and instant coffee. Fold in the egg whites.

Divide the mixture among six small cups or glasses. Chill the cups for 3 hours before serving. Makes 6 servings.

# Chocolate Orange Mousse

*I learned this recipe from a cook in Tampa, Florida, who calls it her "mousse formula of fours," for obvious reasons. I added the liqueur. Garnish this with mandarin orange segments and whipped cream. If you want to skip the orange flavor, substitute 2 teaspoons vanilla extract for the liqueur.*

Melt the chocolate over very low heat. Let it cool to room temperature. Meanwhile, beat the yolks with the sugar and whipping cream. Stir in the melted chocolate and the liqueur. Whip the egg whites until they form soft peaks and fold them into the chocolate mixture. Transfer the mousse to individual glasses or a 4-cup mold. Makes 4 to 6 servings.

*Substitutions and additions:* Instead of orange-based liqueur, use brandy or any other flavored liqueur. Grind ¼ cup walnuts or almonds to a powder in a food processor or blender and stir them into the chocolate-egg yolk mixture before folding in the whites. Or use a food processor to chop ⅓ cup flaked coconut to a powder and substitute rum for the liqueur. Garnish the mousse accordingly.

4 ounces semisweet or bittersweet chocolate (not chips)
4 eggs, separated
4 tablespoons sugar
4 tablespoons whipping cream
2 tablespoons orange liqueur (Cointreau, triple sec, Grand Marnier)

# Light Honey Mousse

*After a spicy or hearty dinner, this sweet, light, semi-hard frozen mousse is especially good. Serve it with gingersnaps or crisp chocolate cookies.*

6 egg yolks
¾ cup honey
2 teaspoons vanilla
3 egg whites
½ cup whipping cream

Combine the egg yolks and honey in a large bowl and beat with an electric mixer for about 5 minutes. The mixture should be thick, foamy, pale, and more than doubled in volume. In a clean bowl with clean beaters, beat the egg whites until they begin to stand in stiff peaks.

Proceed immediately to the cream (using the egg white beaters if you wish; no need to wash them), and beat until it stands in stiff peaks also. Scoop the whipped cream and egg whites on top of the honey mixture and fold together until there are no drifts of unblended white. Scoop into individual stemmed glasses or a large bowl, cover with plastic, and freeze for several hours before serving. Makes about 2 quarts or 10 servings.

P.S. Use the extra egg yolks in mayonnaise or hollandaise.

# Mocha Ricotta

*A sweet, Italianesque ricotta dessert, flecked with grated chocolate and pulverized coffee, takes only a few minutes to make in a food processor— or to blend by hand. It is really better if made the day before.*

Combine all the ingredients in a mixing bowl or food processor. Blend until thoroughly combined. Cover and refrigerate for at least an hour or overnight. Serve with crisp, thin "water crackers" (such as Carr's Table Wafers) or butter biscuits (such as Petite Beurre) and fresh pears or stewed fruit. This is delicious as a filling between cake layers; frost the exterior with whipped cream sprinkled with cocoa and pulverized coffee. Makes about 2 cups.

1 pound (1½ cups) ricotta
½ cup sugar
1 to 2 tablespoons brandy
2 tablespoons pulverized coffee (as fine as powder)
1 square (1 ounce) unsweetened chocolate, finely grated

# Mocha Sponge

*A sponge is similar to a mousse, but lighter and less filling. This one, a bittersweet mixture of chocolate and coffee, is pretty served in stemmed glasses and topped with a spoonful of whipped cream.*

2 cups cold coffee
2 squares (2 ounces) unsweetened
    chocolate, finely grated
2 envelopes unflavored gelatin
½ cup sugar
3 egg whites
½ cup whipping cream

Place the coffee and chocolate in a medium-size, heavy saucepan. Sprinkle with the gelatin and let stand for 5 minutes to soften. Bring just to a simmer over medium heat, whisking almost constantly, to dissolve the gelatin and smooth the melting chocolate—but don't let it boil. Add the sugar and stir until it dissolves. Remove from heat and chill until the mixture is as thick as unbeaten egg whites.

In a clean bowl, beat the egg whites until stiff. With the same beaters—no need to wash them—whip the cream until stiff also. Fold the beaten egg whites and cream into the partially thickened coffee mixture until there are no unblended drifts of white. Spoon into individual stemmed glasses and chill at least 2 hours, until set. Serve with additional whipped cream, if you wish. Makes 6 servings.

# Irish Coffee Gel

*The flavors of the classic San Francisco drink make a good gelatin dessert, too.*

**S**prinkle the gelatin over the whiskey in a small bowl to soften it. After a few minutes, pour on the boiling water to dissolve it. Stir in the sugar until it dissolves. Add the coffee and vanilla.

Pour the mixture into 6 individual serving dishes, wine glasses, custard cups, or Irish coffee glasses. Chill for several hours or overnight, or until set. Serve with whipped cream and, if you like, a grating of bittersweet chocolate. Makes 6 servings.

**1 envelope unflavored gelatin**
**¼ cup Irish whiskey, bourbon, or brandy**
**½ cup boiling water**
**½ cup sugar**
**2 cups cold strong coffee**
**½ teaspoon vanilla extract**

---

**Q.** *How long can I keep leftover egg whites or egg yolks?*

**A.** Leftover egg whites keep beautifully in the freezer. I use an old ice cube tray. One egg white just about fills one of the compartments. When the egg whites are frozen solid, transfer them to a plastic freezer bag to keep them from dehydrating. Thaw them at room temperature and use them for angel food cakes, soufflés, and mousses. They won't whip quite as high as fresh eggs, but just use an extra one. Egg whites frozen this way will keep for a year or more.

Egg yolks are more of a problem. They can be frozen in little cups—the kind you use for taking a sip of water are perfect—covered with water. When the ice melts, you can just pour the liquid off.

# Banana Cantaloupe Gel

*Before there was flavored Jell-O, there was fresh fruit thickened with gelatin. We can forget how good such simple fare can be.*

**4 teaspoons (about 1½ envelopes)
   unflavored gelatin**
**⅓ cup water**
**3 bananas**
**1 cantaloupe**
**⅓ cup sugar**
**Juice of 2 lemons**
**Pinch salt**

Sprinkle the gelatin over the water in a small cup and let soften for several minutes.

Peel the bananas, break them into 2-inch chunks, and put them into the food processor. Halve the cantaloupe, scoop out the seeds, and scrape the orange flesh away from the rind. Drop the peeled and seeded cantaloupe into the processor with the bananas. Puree until smooth, then pour into a bowl. Add the sugar, lemon juice, and salt, and stir until you feel no granules of sugar on your tongue when you taste the mixture.

Place the softened gelatin in a small pan over medium heat and stir until melted, or cover and microwave on full power for 30 seconds. In either case, it should just melt, not boil. Whisk the melted gelatin into the fruit mixture. Gently put a piece of plastic wrap directly on the surface of the gel (so the top doesn't turn brownish) and chill until set—at which time the plastic wrap will peel off easily. This is especially good with whipped cream and crisp gingersnaps. Makes 6 servings.

# Lemon Jelly

*Spread this golden, not-too-sweet jelly on crisp toast with coffee or tea. It is also delicious with pancakes, French toast, and biscuits. The amount is small, but the recipe can easily be doubled. It is also made the old-fashioned way, without commercial pectin. Smooth, round Meyer lemons, which are less tart than other varieties, are especially good.*

Slice the lemons thin, including the rind, seeds, and all, and place in a saucepan. Core the apples, but do not peel them, and chop coarsely. Add to the pan. Pour in sufficient water just to cover the fruit—about 1½ to 2 cups. Cook gently over medium heat for about 15 minutes, until the fruit is soft. Pour into a jelly bag or a colander lined with several thicknesses of damp cheesecloth and let drip into a bowl for about an hour.

Measure the juice; you should have about 2 cups. For each cup of juice, add ¾ cup of sugar. Return to the pan and boil for another 10 to 15 minutes, until the mixture reaches the "jelly" stage—about 220° F. to 225° F. on a candy thermometer. To check, place a tablespoon of the hot mixture on a saucer and set in the freezer for a few minutes—if it jells, the mixture is ready. Pour the jelly into hot, sterilized jars and seal, or store in a covered container in the refrigerator for several months. Makes 2 cups.

6 lemons (about 1 pound)
2 large, tart apples
Water
About 1½ cups sugar

LOW CALORIE · LOW FAT ·

# Blueberry "Pudding"

*Based on a recipe from a listener, who calls her recipe, "Edward's Blueberry Pudding," this is not a pudding per se but more like a cake-topped deep-dish blueberry pie. The upside-down custard cup is critical because, as the dish cools, the cup sucks up the excess moisture from the baked blueberries.*

2 pint baskets fresh or frozen
   blueberries
About 2 tablespoons sugar

Cake topping:
1 cup flour
1½ teaspoons baking powder
½ teaspoon salt
⅓ cup sugar
1 egg
½ cup milk
½ cup (1 stick) melted butter
½ teaspoon vanilla

Use a deep baking pan, about 4 inches deep. A wide saucepan or a large soufflé mold are reasonable substitutes. Butter a custard cup inside and out using some of the melted butter for the cake. Place it upside down in the middle of the pan or mold.

Pour the blueberries into the pan to a depth of 2 inches. Sprinkle them with the sugar, using more or less depending on the natural sweetness of the blueberries.

Preheat the oven to 400° F.

In a medium-size mixing bowl, combine the flour, baking powder, salt, and sugar. Mix well. Beat the milk and the egg until smooth, then combine with the dry ingredients, melted butter, and vanilla, mixing with a fork to form a thick batter. Pour and scrape this onto the berries.

Bake for 30 to 45 minutes, or until the cake is browned and tests done. (To test the cake, put the knife in about 1 inch deep—any further and you'll hit some berries and get a false reading.)

Let the cake cool for at least 10 or 15 minutes. Then spoon the berries and cake into bowls. No topping is necessary, but ice cream is wonderful with the warm fruit. Makes 6 to 8 servings.

# Berry Pudding

*The idea here is that cake batter rises around the berries to make an attractive dessert, especially with a scoop of vanilla ice cream melting over it.*

Preheat the oven to 350° F.

Beat together ¾ cup of the sugar and the shortening until completely blended. Stir together the flour, baking powder, and salt. Add to the sugar mixture along with the milk. Beat until smooth and well blended. Spread the batter evenly in the bottom of a 2 ½- to 3-quart baking dish.

In another bowl, stir together the remaining 1 cup of sugar with the berries and boiling water. Pour the berry mixture over the batter and bake for about 45 minutes, until puffed and bubbling, and the cake on top springs back when touched gently. Cool a little before serving. This will come from the oven with berries and cake on top, and a sweet, thick berry sauce on the bottom. Serve warm, with vanilla ice cream. Makes 8 servings.

1¾ cups sugar
½ cup vegetable shortening or softened butter
2 cups flour
2 teaspoons baking powder
½ teaspoon salt
1¼ cups milk
3 cups fresh blackberries, blueberries, boysenberries, or raspberries
2 cups boiling water

# Cider Bread Pudding

*The flavors of fall come through in this hearty dessert, accentuated by boiling the cider to concentrate its flavor.*

4 cups apple cider
2 cups milk
½ cup maple syrup
¼ cup cream or half-and-half
5 cups bread cubes or small bits
    (about ½ loaf French bread)
½ cup raisins (optional)
3 eggs, beaten

Boil the cider in a large pan until it is reduced to 1 cup—keep an eye on it, especially near the end, so it doesn't evaporate completely. Remove from heat, add the milk and maple syrup, then return to heat, stirring almost constantly, until the mixture is hot; don't worry if it looks slightly curdled, just keep stirring. Remove from heat and stir in the cream, which will make it smooth again. Pour over the bread cubes, add the raisins if you wish, stir to combine, and let sit 20 minutes.

Preheat the oven to 350° F.

Pour the beaten eggs on the bread mixture and fold them in. Turn the pudding into a buttered 1½- to 2-quart baking dish and set in a larger pan. Add boiling water to the larger pan to come halfway up the sides of the pudding dish. Bake for 45 minutes, until lightly browned on top. Serve warm, with ice cream, or a pitcher of milk or cream. Makes 6 servings.

# Chocolate Cracker Pudding

*Adding chocolate lifts a classic Pennsylvania Dutch cracker pudding into another realm. After chilling, it has a rather pebbly, rough look, but the texture is smooth on your tongue, and it will be just softly set, not as firm as a regular chocolate pudding. Serve with whipped cream or ice cream, if you wish.*

Heat the milk in a heavy saucepan almost to boiling. Meanwhile, beat the egg yolks and sugar together, and whisk into the nearly boiling milk. Add the crumbled crackers and cook over medium heat, stirring constantly, until the mixture boils. Add the coconut and chocolate and stir again until the chocolate melts and the pudding bubbles briskly. Remove from heat.

Beat the egg whites until they stand in soft peaks, then fold into the warm chocolate mixture. Scoop into a large, clear glass bowl (or individual bowls), and chill for several hours before serving. Makes about 2 quarts, serving 6 to 8. Best served fresh, but it will keep in the refrigerator for 3 or 4 days.

4 cups milk

3 eggs, separated

½ cup sugar

2 cups saltine crackers, coarsely crumbled (1 "stack" of crackers)

1 cup shredded coconut

3 squares (3 ounces) unsweetened chocolate, chopped

# Cold Zabaglione

*This is an easy sauce to prepare in advance for an elegant and delicious finish to dinner. I had it served over a poached peach filled with ground nuts. Using a flavorful white wine, such as Muscat or Gewürztraminer, gives it a lighter taste than the traditional Marsala or sherry.*

4 egg yolks
4 teaspoons sugar
¼ cup wine (a sweet Muscat, Gewürztraminer, Riesling, or sherry)
½ cup whipping cream

A copper bowl is the preferred utensil for getting the most air into the zabaglione. Any bowl-shaped pan works well. Double boilers with flat bottoms and vertical sides can scorch the yolks.

In a fairly large bowl—you want room to splash a little—combine the yolks, sugar, and wine. Start beating with a wire whisk or a hand-held electric beater. Place the bowl over low heat or on a pan of simmering water. If you place the bowl over direct heat, you will have to keep taking it off the heat from time to time to keep it from overcooking. Use a pot holder or towel to hold the bowl.

Keep whipping until the yolks multiply in volume and become very light and fluffy. Take off the heat. (This is warm zabaglione and can be served fresh as is.)

In a separate bowl, whip the cream until it forms very soft peaks. It should be about the texture of the zabaglione or softer. Fold this into the slightly cooled zabaglione.

This sauce will keep up to 8 hours in the refrigerator, unlike cream-free zabaglione, which starts to deflate after a few minutes. Makes 8 to 10 servings as a sauce.

# Zabaglione Variations

*This is a quick and easy "emergency" dessert, delicious by itself or served over fresh fruit. The technique is to whip the egg yolks with a wire whisk or an electric mixer while warming the container over low heat. The result is a foamy dessert to be served warm in goblets or over cut-up fruit.*

Separate the eggs and put the yolks in a metal bowl or saucepan. The best shape is rounded so the whisk can catch all the egg as it foams up. (Save the whites for future use.) Use half of an eggshell to measure the liquid into the yolks (or measure 1 tablespoons per yolk). Add the sugar.

Start whisking the yolks, holding the bowl over low heat with a pot holder to protect your hands as the bowl heats up. Continue whisking until the yolks balloon to eight or nine times their original volume. Serve warm or cold over fresh fruit.

**For each serving:**
**1 egg yolk**
**1 teaspoon sugar**
**Your choice of flavorful liquid:**
  **Marsala (traditional), sweet sherry, liqueur, brandy, dessert wine, or fresh orange juice**

---

Q. *What is a simple way to make* crème fraîche?

A. *Crème fraîche* has long been popular in France, where dairies make it regularly, the way ours make sour cream. When French cooking started becoming popular, a couple of recipes appeared that used buttermilk or sour cream with whipping cream to make what was called *crème fraîche*. These products are tasty, but they do not have the most important property of true *crème fraîche*, its ability to thicken sauces without breaking or curdling.

True *crème fraîche* culture is available from dairy supply stores. Use it the same way you use yogurt culture, except use it on cream instead of milk.

# Strawberry Tapioca Trifle

*This twist on a traditional British dessert uses fresh strawberries and homemade tapioca pudding rather than gobs of* crème anglaise *and whipped cream.*

⅓ cup quick-cooking tapioca
¾ cup sugar
3 eggs, separated
3 cups milk
2 teaspoons vanilla
3 pint baskets ripe strawberries, stemmed and sliced
1 pound cake (12 to 16 ounces), thinly sliced
½ cup brandy
½ cup toasted sliced almonds (optional garnish)

Combine the tapioca, ¼ cup of the sugar, the egg yolks, and milk in a saucepan and whisk until blended. Let stand 5 minutes. Cook over moderate heat, whisking constantly, until the mixture comes to a full boil. Set aside.

In a separate bowl, beat the egg whites to soft peaks, then add the vanilla and ¼ cup of the remaining sugar; beat until stiff peaks form. Stir the hot tapioca mixture into the beaten whites. Let cool to room temperature.

Meanwhile, toss the sliced berries with the remaining ¼ cup of sugar and mash them slightly. Set aside.

Line the bottom of a clear glass bowl of at least 3-quart capacity with half the cake slices, and sprinkle with ¼ cup of the brandy. Spoon on half the berries and their juices and spread with half the tapioca. Repeat the layers, ending with tapioca. Chill several hours before serving; garnish with toasted sliced almonds, if you wish. Makes 4 servings.

# Rice Pudding

*This is an adaptation of an old-fashioned baked version. I prefer to cook it on top of the stove. Use a thick saucepan over very low heat so it doesn't scorch. If you're nervous about scorching, use a double boiler. For those who don't want to use a vanilla bean, stir 1 tablespoon of vanilla extract into the pudding as you take it off the heat.*

In a heavy saucepan or the top of a double boiler, combine all the ingredients except the eggs. Bring the mixture to a simmer over boiling water. Let it cook, uncovered, until the rice is very soft, about 1 hour. Stir it occasionally. Blend in the eggs and let the pudding cook for about 15 minutes longer, stirring it occasionally.

Remove the vanilla bean and dry it for further use. Refrigerate the pudding. Makes 4 servings.

4 cups milk
⅔ cup sugar
⅓ cup uncooked white rice
1 vanilla bean
Grated zest of 1 lemon (the yellow part of the rind)
⅓ cup blanched almonds, coarsely chopped
2 eggs

# Orange Omelet

*For informal meals, you could make individual dessert omelets 2 or 3 eggs at a time, but if you have a large enough pan, 1 large omelet makes a cozier presentation. A 12-inch nonstick omelet pan is useful for things other than omelets—sautéing large quantities of onions or pan-grilling fish fillets, for example.*

12 eggs
¼ cup granulated sugar
½ cup Cointreau (or other orange liqueur)
4 tablespoons butter
½ cup orange marmalade
1 orange for decoration

Combine eggs and sugar in a bowl, whisking them together. Flavor with ¼ cup of the orange liqueur and mix well. Fill a china or tempered glass bowl with boiling water to warm it. Empty and dry the bowl. Put marmalade in warm bowl to soften it, add the remainder of the orange liqueur, and lightly mix.

Melt butter in a 12-inch omelet pan (preferably non-stick) over medium heat. When butter is just golden, add the eggs. Bring in the edges with a wooden spatula to prevent burning.

When the omelet is cooked but not dried out, remove from heat and spread on most of the marmalade, saving 2 tablespoons for the top.

To serve, slide half of the omelet onto a serving dish, then fold over the other half by turning the pan over. Spread the rest of the marmalade over the omelet. Decorate with slices of orange. Serves 4 or 5.

# Bittersweet Chocolate Flake Ice Cream

*Adding warm melted chocolate to a cool cream mixture hardens the chocolate immediately, magically creating chocolate flakes. This recipe makes a half-gallon.*

In a blender or food processor, combine the yolks, vanilla, cocoa, sugar, and 1 cup of the half-and-half. Blend it smooth. Meanwhile, melt the chocolate in the top of a double boiler or in a bowl in a microwave oven. Stop the blender, pour the chocolate in, and wait a few seconds before turning it on again. Turn it on for several seconds to chop up the chocolate.

Pour the mixture into a half-gallon ice-cream maker, and add the remaining half-and-half and the cream. Stir well and freeze according to the machine's directions. Makes ½ gallon.

3 egg yolks
1 tablespoon vanilla
½ cup unsweetened cocoa
2 cups sugar
4 cups half-and-half
8 squares (8 ounces) bittersweet or semisweet chocolate
1 cup whipping cream

**Q.** *Every time I make ice cream it tastes great until I put it in the freezer. Then it gets terribly icy. What am I doing wrong?*

**A.** You're not doing anything wrong. It's just that we have all become accustomed to commercial ice creams, which contain emulsifiers such as carageenan and agar gum to keep them from turning icy when frozen solid. Egg is also an emulsifier, and any ice-cream recipe containing egg should not turn icy. Homemade ice cream doesn't need emulsifiers if it is eaten before it freezes solid.

**Q.** *How far in advance can I ice a cake with whipped cream?*

**A.** When you ice a cake with whipped cream, it should be kept refrigerated if you plan to serve it more than an hour or two later. Whipped cream icing is delicate and often loses its texture if applied too soon. To keep it longer, try softening a packet of unflavored gelatin in ¼ cup water, dissolving it over low heat or in the microwave oven, and adding 1 teaspoon of this mixture to each cup of whipping cream.

# Chocolate Chestnut Ice Cream

*Smooth and chocolaty, with a delicate chestnut flavor, this ice cream is good topped with a spoonful of unsweetened whipped cream and some shaved chocolate. Cooked chestnut puree can be purchased in cans or jars or made from fresh roasted chestnuts.*

Combine the chocolate chips and milk in a pan, and stir over low heat until melted and smooth. Beat the eggs and sugar together in a bowl, and whisk in the hot chocolate mixture. Then add the chestnut puree and whisk until smooth. Stir in the cream and vanilla and chill the mixture. Freeze in an ice-cream maker, following its directions. Makes about 1½ quarts.

1 cup semisweet chocolate chips
1½ cups milk
2 eggs
½ cup sugar
1 cup cooked chestnut puree
1½ cups whipping cream
2 teaspoons vanilla

# Chocolate Malt Ice Cream

*This tastes very much like the frozen chocolate malts once popular at fairs and carnivals. You still find them at baseball games. This rather light ice cream is smooth and not too sweet. Malted milk powder is found in the sugar and syrup section of the grocery. You might have to ask your grocer for it.*

In a bowl, stir the sugar and cornstarch together until blended, then beat in the eggs. Combine the milk and chocolate in a saucepan, and set over medium heat, stirring frequently, until melted and smooth. Slowly whisk into the sugar and egg mixture, then return to the saucepan and place back over heat, stirring constantly, for 2 minutes—do not let it boil. Refrigerate, stirring occasionally, until chilled. Add the malt powder and cream and stir until smooth. Freeze in an ice-cream freezer, according to the machine's directions. Makes about 1 quart.

½ cup sugar
2 teaspoons cornstarch
2 eggs
2 cups milk
2 squares (2 ounces) unsweetened chocolate, chopped
⅔ cup malted milk powder
¾ cup whipping cream

# Cheesecake Ice Cream

*Inspired by the buttermilk milk shakes at The Diner in Napa Valley, which tasted like liquid cheesecake to me, my version is an ice cream that tastes like cheesecake, with no cheese in it. (Or cake, for that matter.)*

**4 egg yolks**
**2 cups whipping cream**
**1 cup sugar**
**Pinch salt**
**½ lemon**
**1½ teaspoons vanilla extract**
**2 cups buttermilk**

Place in a bowl the egg yolks, 1 cup of the cream, sugar, salt, the grated zest of the lemon, and the vanilla. Blend with a whisk until smooth. Add the remaining cup of cream, and the lemon juice and buttermilk. Stir the mixture and chill.

Freeze in an ice-cream freezer according to manufacturer's directions. You can add 1 cup of crushed and sugared fruit, if desired. Makes ½ gallon.

**Q.** *I bought a huge bottle of vanilla from Mexico, but my friend told me you said it wasn't safe. What's the story?*

**A.** Mexican labeling laws are not as strictly enforced as ours, and it's common to see large bottles of "vanilla" being sold in Mexico for very low prices. The reason the stuff is so cheap is that it is cut with coumarin, an extract of the tonka tree that smells like vanilla and is much cheaper to make. The mixture in cheap "vanilla" could be 80 percent coumarin. Unfortunately, it has been shown to cause bladder tumors in experimental animals. Although some recent experiments have shown no toxic effects on humans in the concentrations found in Mexican vanilla, why take a chance?

Mexican vanilla bought in the United States is regulated by the FDA. Independent tests have shown it to be pure vanilla.

# Fruit Ice Cream Formula

*The lack of eggs for emulsification makes a delightfully fresh and pure tasting ice cream, but it won't keep for long. Eat it straight from the ice-cream machine. Use fruit such as berries, melons, mangos, papayas, peaches, or pears, but not citrus or dried fruits.*

Ⅰn a 2-quart ice-cream freezer, combine the cream, milk, sugar, and vanilla. Start the machine; when the mixture has begun to thicken, after about 15 minutes, add the fruit. Continue freezing the ice cream until the machine slows or stops.

Because this ice cream has no emulsifiers, it must be eaten the same day or within a day or two. It cannot be kept longer without developing ice crystals.

1½ cups whipping cream or heavy cream
1½ cups milk
1½ cups sugar
1½ teaspoons vanilla
1½ cups mashed or pureed fruit

---

Q. *My peach tree is going crazy. I like to make peach pies, but what is the best way to freeze them?*

A. Here is a neat trick for freezing fruit for pies. Line a pie pan with freezer-going plastic wrap, allowing plenty of extra wrap to drape over the sides. Cut the fruit and toss it with sugar, seasonings, and thickener according to the recipe you like to use. Fill the plastic-lined pie tin, heaping up the fruit as you would in a pie shell. Bring the edges of the plastic up to seal the top. Put the pie tin in the freezer until it freezes solid. Slip the frozen pie-shaped mass of fruit out of the pan and wrap it tightly in freezer wrap. Repeat for as many pies as you like.

To make a pie, roll out the crust as you would normally, slip the pie-shaped frozen fruit into the crust, dot it with butter, and top it with the second crust. Flute and decorate the crust as you normally do. Allow an extra 10 minutes baking time.

# Vanilla Frozen Yogurt

*You can't turn around in any American city these days without encountering a soft-frozen yogurt stand. Ever want to make your own? Here is how.*

1 envelope unflavored gelatin
¼ cup cold water
2 eggs
¼ cup sugar
⅓ cup light corn syrup
2 teaspoons vanilla
2 cups plain yogurt

In a small saucepan, sprinkle the gelatin over the cold water to soften for 5 minutes, then stir it over very low heat until it dissolves.

Beat the eggs until they are light, then add the sugar gradually, beating the mixture until it is light and pale. Gradually beat in the corn syrup. Stir in the vanilla and the yogurt, and, finally, the gelatin.

Turn the mixture into a 1- or 2-quart ice-cream freezer. Freeze it, following the manufacturer's directions. Serve it right out of the freezer while it is still soft. If it must be stored, keep it frozen, but set it in the refrigerator for a few minutes to soften before serving. Makes 4 servings.

# Strawberry Mango Sherbet

*Mangos, used either alone or in combination with other fruits in sherbet, impart a smooth, creamy richness—without the addition of any milk or cream. In this pale orange sherbet, neither fruit dominates the other. The shot of tequila—just enough for a bit of flavor and fragrance—is optional.*

Wash and stem the strawberries. Peel the mangos, then use a sharp knife to cut the flesh from the fibrous pit as best you can—some pits are more fibrous and stubborn than others. Puree the fruits together in a food processor until smooth, then scrape into a bowl. Add the sugar, lemon juice, and tequila or water and stir about 1 minute—until you feel no granules of sugar on your tongue when you taste it. (I've never liked to whip up brightly colored fruit mixtures in the food processor for long; they fade and become pale—maybe because air is whipped into them. That's why I scrape it into a bowl.) Freeze the mixture in an ice-cream maker, according to manufacturer's instructions. Makes about 1 quart.

1 pint basket (about 2 cups) strawberries
3 mangos (about 1½ pounds)
¾ cup sugar
¼ cup lemon juice
¼ cup tequila or water (water simply thins the mixture)

# Rhubarb Sorbet

*Rhubarb has long been known as "pie plant," because after a long winter, it was the first produce harvested that could make a pie—a sign that spring had arrived. It also makes a delicious, pale pink, slightly tart sorbet, with a soft, light texture, somewhat like a frozen mousse. It can be frozen in an automatic ice-cream machine or in the freezer compartment of your refrigerator.*

6 cups (about 3 pounds) thinly sliced rhubarb stalks (not the poisonous leaves)
1¼ cups sugar
1½ cups water
Pinch salt
2 egg whites

Place the rhubarb in a medium saucepan with 1 cup of the sugar and the water. Bring to a boil, reduce heat, and simmer gently for about 5 minutes, until rhubarb is tender. Remove from heat and puree mixture in a blender or food processor. Refrigerate for a few hours, or overnight, until cold.

Place the salt and egg whites in a medium bowl, and beat until they stand in soft peaks. Sprinkle on the remaining ¼ cup of sugar, and continue beating until whites stand in peaks that droop slightly when the beater is lifted. Fold in the chilled rhubarb mixture.

Either freeze according to manufacturer's instructions in an automatic freezing machine, or freeze in the freezer compartment of your refrigerator as follows: Turn the mixture into a shallow pan and set it in the freezer until mushy and almost set (an hour or so if freezer is very cold). Scrape into a mixing bowl and beat furiously until soft and fluffy. Cover and return to freezer until firm enough to scoop. If it is very hard, let set at room temperature a few minutes before serving. Makes 6 to 8 servings.

# Cranberry Ginger Sorbet

*This makes a light and refreshing dessert, especially when served with crisp nut cookies. Squeezing the cranberry syrup through a cheesecloth leaves the slightly astringent cranberry skins behind; that's why it's better not to simply puree the mixture in a food processor. Kelly Mills, chef of the Four Seasons Clift Hotel, created this recipe.*

LOW CALORIE · LOW FAT ·

In a medium-size saucepan, bring the ingredients to a boil, and cook until the berries have fallen apart, about 20 minutes. Cool a little and then strain through cheesecloth. Squeeze out the last few drops of liquid. Freeze the mixture in an ice-cream machine, according to its directions.

Scoop the sorbet into wine glasses, and serve with a mint sprig and assorted nut cookies on the side. Makes ½ gallon.

1 bag (12 ounces) cranberries
2 tablespoons fresh ginger, peeled and diced
3 cups sugar
4 cups water
Juice of 1 Meyer lemon or 2 tablespoons grapefruit juice

# Harvey's Baked Apples

*The secret to great baked apples is in the apples you buy. Firm, deep-red Rome Beauties are my favorites because they bake up with a creamy texture and rich flavor and don't deflate as they cook. Try these for breakfast.*

6 large Rome Beauty or Jonathan
   apples
3 cinnamon sticks, broken in half
⅓ cup golden raisins
3 teaspoons currant jelly
1 cup water
1 tablespoon butter
½ teaspoon ground allspice

Preheat the oven to 325° F.

Core the apples and peel the stem end only. Arrange the apples in a baking pan. Place a half cinnamon stick in each core and fill the rest of the hole with a mixture of raisins and currant jelly. Add the water to the pan. Divide the butter into six pieces. Place a piece of butter on top of each apple and sprinkle the exposed surface with allspice.

Bake the apples, covered with foil, for 45 minutes, or until they are soft. Drain off the liquid and sweeten it to taste to pour over the apples, if you like. Eat them plain or top with a dollop of cream, sour cream, or ice cream. Serve warm or room temperature, not chilled. Makes 6 servings.

# Antique Apples

*I don't know if this preparation is an antique, but the beautiful color these apples take on from cooking in the tea is as appealing as the finest Chippendale table. The idea is from Cornelius O'Donnell.*

LOW CALORIE · LOW FAT ·

In a 2½-quart saucepan, bring 4 cups of water to a boil. Remove from heat and add the tea bags, sugar, spices, and lemon zest. Let stand 5 minutes.

Meanwhile, peel, core, and quarter the apples. Remove the tea bags and bring the liquid to a boil again. Cook the apples in this liquid for 5 minutes, or until they are just cooked through. Remove them with a slotted spoon and place them in a serving dish to cool.

In a small saucepan, combine the marmalade and orange liqueur. (If you don't want to use liqueur, use 2 tablespoons of the liquid from the apples.) Bring to a simmer, stirring well. Pour sauce over the apples. Cut the lemon slices into quarters and scatter them over the apples to garnish. Makes 6 servings.

2 tea bags (not herb or flavored tea)
1 cup sugar
Pinch cinnamon
Pinch ginger
2 strips lemon zest
3 pounds Golden Delicious or Gravenstein apples
½ cup orange marmalade
2 tablespoons orange liqueur (Cointreau, Grand Marnier, triple sec)
4 lemon slices (garnish)

# Harvey's Fruit Compote

*The trick to this dish is to know which fruits cook the fastest and add them last. No fruit takes longer than 5 minutes, so once you make the syrup, the mixture comes together very quickly. Serve it with vanilla ice cream. Use apple or grape juice as the base, or something more unusual, such as currant or pomegranate.*

1 cup bottled fruit juice
½ cup wine, red or white
½ cup sugar
2 pounds mixed fresh fruit and
   berries
½ teaspoon vanilla
2 tablespoons unsalted butter

In a nonreactive saucepan (one without exposed aluminum or iron), combine the fruit juice, wine, and sugar. Bring to a boil to dissolve the sugar. Set aside.

Peel, pit, and slice any stone fruit. Wash and dry any berries. Cut large strawberries into thick slices.

Five minutes before serving, bring the syrup to a boil. Add the fruit, hard fruits first, then progressively softer ones. Berries need only cook for 30 seconds. Add the vanilla and butter. Swirl the mixture until the butter has melted. Spoon into bowls and add a scoop of vanilla ice cream. Makes 6 servings.

# Red Poached Pears

*Cooking the pears in red wine turns them a beautiful color, and using the poaching liquid in the sauce makes it just as pretty and tasty.*

Peel and core the pears, leaving them whole. Boil the wine, sugar, and cinnamon stick together in a medium saucepan for 5 minutes. Reduce the heat and drop in the pears; if they are not almost completely covered with liquid, add a little water. Cover and simmer gently until the pears are tender when pierced, about 30 minutes. If you have the time, let the pears steep in the liquid, off heat, for several hours or overnight before continuing—the longer they sit, the deeper their color. Remove the pears and arrange stem-end up in a clear glass bowl.

When you are ready to make the sauce, boil the poaching liquid down rapidly over high heat until it is reduced to 1 cup. Meanwhile, whisk the egg yolks in a small bowl until they are pale yellow. Whisk the hot reduced wine into the yolks, then return the mixture to the saucepan. Place over moderate heat, stirring constantly, until the sauce becomes very light, foamy, and slightly thickened—but does not boil. Then pour it over the pears and let sit until serving time. If the wait is more than a couple of hours, refrigerate and serve cold. Makes 4 servings.

**4 firm, ripe Bosc pears**
**1 bottle dry red wine**
**½ cup sugar**
**1 cinnamon stick**
**3 egg yolks**

# Blueberry Tart

*A summertime visit to the Coach House in New York inspired this recipe's delicious combination of cooked and fresh blueberries. For a blueberry lover like me, it is the best of both worlds. The tart looks (and tastes) good with a dollop of whipped cream on each serving.*

**Cookie crust:**

1½ cups cookie crumbs (vanilla wafers, gingersnaps, or butter cookies)

½ cup (1 stick) melted butter

½ cup sugar

**Filling:**

2 pint baskets fresh blueberries

⅓ cup sugar

1 lemon

½ teaspoon cinnamon

1 cup pastry cream (*crème patissière*) or sweetened whipped cream

**Pastry cream:**

¾ cup milk

¼ cup sugar

2 yolks of extra-large eggs

2 tablespoons flour

½ teaspoon vanilla

To make the cookie crust: Blend all the ingredients together to make a paste. Press it evenly into a 9-inch tart tin or pie pan. Bake 5 minutes at 350° F. Let cool.

To make the filling: Pick over the berries to remove all the little stems and green berries. Set aside 2½ cups of the best-looking berries.

In a saucepan, combine the remaining 1½ cups of berries and the sugar. Grate 1 teaspoon of the lemon peel and squeeze in about 1 teaspoon of lemon juice. Add the cinnamon and bring the mixture slowly to a boil. Raise the heat and boil the berries for 8 minutes, or until the mixture resembles jam. Set it aside to cool.

To make the pastry cream: Bring the milk to a simmer in a small saucepan. In a small bowl, with a wire whisk, whip the sugar and egg yolks until the mixture is very smooth and thick. Whisk in the flour. Strain the hot milk into the egg mixture, beating with the whisk. Pour the mixture into the saucepan. Bring it to a boil, whisking constantly, then boil for 1 minute, stirring constantly. Add the vanilla. Let the pastry cream cool before using it. Makes 1 cup.

To assemble the tart: Spread the pastry cream or sweetened whipped cream over the cooled crust. Top it with the cooled jam and finally with the fresh blueberries. Refrigerate the tart until serving time. Makes 8 servings.

# Buttery Thin Lemon Tart

*A very rich, tart lemon custard fills a tart shell to make an elegant dessert with the homey touch of a final broiling, which always seems to brown it somewhat evenly.*

Preheat the oven to 400° F.

Bake the shell for 10 to 15 minutes. Lower the heat to 350° F. and remove the shell to cool slightly while you prepare the filling. (The shell may puff unevenly; for this recipe it doesn't matter.)

Melt the butter and set it aside to cool a bit. In a mixing bowl, beat together the sugar and eggs until they are very smooth and pale. Add the zest, then stir in the melted butter. Whisk in the lemon juice gradually.

Pour this mixture into the prepared shell. Bake it for 20 to 25 minutes, or until the filling is set and a knife inserted near the center comes out dry. Remove the shell from the oven while the broiler preheats.

Broil the tart until it turns a golden, spotty brown. Watch it constantly, because this only takes a few seconds. Remove it immediately and let it cool. This is best served slightly warm or at room temperature. Makes 6 to 8 servings.

A 9-inch tart shell or pie shell (page 298)

½ cup (1 stick) butter

⅔ cup sugar

3 eggs

1 tablespoon grated lemon zest (the yellow part of the peel)

¾ cup lemon juice, strained

# Pear Tarte Tatin

*The classic French upside-down fruit tart,* Tarte Tatin, *is made with apples, but firm, crisp pears make a welcome change of pace. Crisp Bosc pears are best for this recipe, but other less firm varieties also work. (Try substituting ¼ cup of cornmeal for ¼ cup of the flour in your regular pie dough recipe. This goes especially well with pears.)*

**6 large pears (about 4 pounds), firm but ripe**
**¾ cup sugar**
**1 lemon**
**3 tablespoons water**
**Basic pie or tart dough for a 9-inch pie shell (page 298)**

Peel and core the pears and cut them into eighths. Toss in a large bowl with ¼ cup of the sugar. Grate in the zest of the lemon, then squeeze in the lemon's juice and toss again. Set aside for at least 45 minutes, so the pears exude some of their juices.

Meanwhile, combine the remaining ½ cup of the sugar and the water in a heavy skillet with an ovenproof handle, such as a cast-iron one, about 9 inches in diameter. Set over high heat and boil rapidly for several minutes, swirling the pan occasionally, until the mixture turns a deep, caramel brown. Remove from heat and set aside until the caramel hardens.

Preheat the oven to 450° F.

Drain the pears, reserving any juices, and arrange them in a neat pattern in the caramel, mounding them up in the center. Roll the dough into a circle slightly larger than the skillet and lay it over the pears, tucking it down inside the pan. Cut several vents on top. Bake for about 40 minutes, until bubbling and the pears are tender when pierced. Remove from the oven and let sit for 10 minutes.

Depending on what kind of pears you use, you're apt to have some sweet, caramel colored juices around the edge. Draw the juice out as best you can with a bulb baster, and combine with the reserved pear juices. Unmold the tart by deftly inverting the skillet onto a large platter. Serve it warm, along with whipped cream or ice cream, and pass the combined juices as a ready-made sauce. Makes 6 servings.

# Mango Chiffon Pie

*This is incredible—light as a cloud, not too sweet—and it tastes like fresh mangos. The quivery filling is just firm enough to cut, so keep it chilled until serving.*

Peel and pit the mangos; puree the pulp in a blender or food processor. You should have 1½ cups of puree. Sprinkle the gelatin over the water in a small cup, and let stand a few minutes to soften. Beat the lemon juice, egg yolks, and ¼ cup of the sugar together in a small saucepan. Set over moderate heat and whisk constantly for a few minutes until hot, foamy, and thick, but do not boil. Add the softened gelatin and whisk over heat for about 30 seconds more. Remove from heat, stir in the mango puree, and pour into a bowl. Refrigerate, stirring occasionally, until the mixture just begins to hold its shape and mounds slightly when dropped from a spoon.

Beat the egg whites until they form soft peaks, then add the remaining ¼ cup of the sugar and the salt, and continue beating until the egg whites are stiff and shiny. In another bowl, whip the cream until it forms soft peaks. Fold both the whipped cream and egg whites into the mango mixture until blended. Mound in the pie shell and chill for several hours. Makes 6 servings.

2 large mangos
1 envelope unflavored gelatin
¼ cup cold water
¼ cup lemon juice
4 eggs, separated
½ cup sugar
⅔ cup whipping cream
Pinch salt
A 9-inch fully baked pie shell (page 298)

# Orange Rhubarb Pie

*The rhubarb and oranges retain their fresh flavors in this colorful and delicious pie. It is very juicy, though, and tapioca is a fine thickener, because the thickened juices remain clear; flour turns them a very pasty white.*

Basic pie pastry for a 2-crust 9-inch
    pie (page 298)
4 large navel oranges (about 2
    pounds)
4 cups rhubarb stalks (about 1 large
    bunch), leaves removed, cut into
    ½-inch pieces
1¼ cups sugar
2½ tablespoons quick-cooking
    tapioca
Pinch salt
2 tablespoons butter

Preheat the oven to 450° F.

Line a 9-inch pie pan with half the rolled-out pastry dough. Roll out the remaining dough for a top crust, and set it aside on a piece of wax paper or a floured surface.

With a sharp knife, peel the oranges, exposing the flesh all around and removing the bitter white part. Cut between each membrane to remove the orange segments, dropping them into a bowl as you work. Add the rhubarb and toss to mix. In a small bowl, stir together the sugar, tapioca, and salt to combine, then pour over the fruit and toss again until completely coated. Pile the fruit into the dough-lined pan and dot with the butter. Cover with the top crust, cut a few steam vents in the top crust, and trim and crimp the edges.

Bake for about 15 minutes, until the crust has begun to brown, then reduce heat to 350° F. and bake about 30 minutes longer, until the juices are bubbling and the pie is well browned. Serve warm or at room temperature, with vanilla ice cream, if you wish. Makes 6 servings.

# Peanut Butter Pie

*This is a variation on a recipe a listener sent in when I couldn't come up with a quick recipe for another listener's request. It turns out to be a very different approach, one that has become a favorite around our house.*

Combine the sugar, flour, and a pinch of salt in a saucepan and mix well. Blend in the milk gradually. Bring the mixture to a boil, then reduce heat to cook, stirring the mixture constantly until smooth and very thick, 3 to 5 minutes. Remove from heat.

In a small bowl, beat the egg yolks and gradually stir in ½ cup of the hot mixture. Return the yolk mixture to the pan and cook 2 minutes. Remove from heat and stir in vanilla. Cool to room temperature. Every now and then, give it a stir as it cools.

Preheat the oven to 375° F.

In another bowl, mix the powdered sugar and peanut butter with a fork until crumbly. Spread half of the peanut butter mixture over the bottom of the pastry shell. Pour the cooled filling over it. Top with the remaining peanut butter mixture.

Beat the egg whites until they form stiff peaks. Spread this over the filling. Bake the pie until the meringue is brown, about 8 minutes. Cool to room temperature. Makes 6 servings.

½ cup sugar
½ cup flour
Pinch salt
2 ¼ cups milk
3 eggs, separated
1 teaspoon vanilla
½ cup powdered sugar, sifted
½ cup peanut butter
1 baked 9-inch pastry shell (page 298)

# Persimmon Chiffon Pie

*This spicy pie is lighter than most traditional holiday pies or persimmon puddings. Serve along with a few gingersnap cookies if you wish.*

Fully baked 9-inch pie shell (page
 298) or a 9-inch graham cracker
 crust (page 299)
2 or 3 large ripe persimmons
1 envelope unflavored gelatin
¼ cup cold water
4 eggs, separated
¾ cup brown sugar
2 teaspoons pumpkin pie spice
2 tablespoons sugar
1 cup whipping cream

Have the pie shell ready; if it is a graham cracker crust, chill it thoroughly before filling. Cut the persimmons in half; they should be very soft. Grate them against a coarse grater (the peel will protect your fingers) to make pulp. You should have 1¼ cups pulp.

Sprinkle the gelatin over the water in a small cup and set aside for several minutes while you continue. Place the egg yolks in a medium-size, heavy-bottom pan, and beat briskly with a whisk for about 1 minute. Add the brown sugar, spice, and persimmon pulp. Mix well, then cook over medium heat for about 5 minutes, until mixture is quite hot and you see wisps of steam rising. Do not let it boil. Stir in the softened gelatin and cook for about 1 minute longer, without boiling. Scrape the mixture into a bowl and refrigerate, stirring occasionally, for an hour or so, until it mounds slightly when dropped from a spoon.

Beat the egg whites until foamy, then add the granulated sugar and beat until they stand in soft peaks. At once beat the cream in a separate bowl until it forms soft peaks. Gently fold the beaten egg whites and whipped cream and the cooled persimmon mixture together until well blended. Pile into the prepared pie shell and chill until set—a few hours, or overnight. Makes 6 servings.

# Harvey's Pumpkin Pie

*My version of the classic American holiday dessert uses a custom-blend of fresh spices rather than a prepackaged spice mixture.*

Preheat the oven to 450° F.

Freeze the unbaked pie shell for at least 30 minutes. This is important for the texture of the crust.

Heat the cream and half-and-half in a small saucepan. Meanwhile, in a mixing bowl, beat the eggs with the vanilla, the brown sugar, and spices. Then add the pumpkin puree and mix well. Gradually stir in the hot cream.

Pour the pumpkin mixture into the frozen crust, and immediately put it in the oven. After 10 minutes, reduce the temperature to 350° F., and continue baking the pie for 30 to 40 minutes longer, or until a knife inserted near the middle of the pie comes out clean. Let the pie cool on a rack. Serve it at room temperature or slightly warm, with a dab of sweetened whipped cream. (Use the remaining half cup from the cream container you bought for the pie.) Makes 6 to 8 servings.

If you wish to make pumpkin puree from fresh pumpkin, use small, firm sugar pumpkins, not the large jack-o'-lantern types sold at Halloween. Peel and seed the pumpkin. Cut it into 2- or 3-inch chunks. Put the chunks in a baking pan with a splash of water, cover it tightly, and bake at 375° F. for 40 minutes, or until the pumpkin is soft. Drain it well and puree it in a food processor, blender, or food mill. This puree will keep refrigerated for up to a week or frozen for up to 6 months.

1 9-inch pie shell, in a deep-dish pie pan (page 298)
½ cup whipping cream
1¼ cups half-and-half
3 eggs
½ teaspoon vanilla extract
¾ cup brown sugar
1 teaspoon cinnamon
½ teaspoon ground ginger
½ teaspoon nutmeg
¼ teaspoon allspice
2 cups canned pumpkin puree (1 pound)—not pie filling

# Blum's Coffee-crunch Cake

*During the first year of the "KCBS Kitchen," a caller phoned in with a nostalgic request: How did Blum's make that wonderful crunchy topping for its coffee-crunch cake? As usual, other listeners came to the rescue with several versions of the recipe. This one worked best. (Note: You can prepare the topping a day before serving.)*

**Yellow sponge cake, 10-inch tube shape**

**Topping:**
1½ cups sugar
¼ cup strong hot coffee
¼ cup white corn syrup
1 tablespoon baking soda, sifted
2 cups (1 pint) whipping cream
2 tablespoons sugar
1 teaspoon vanilla

Measure the 1½ cups of sugar, coffee, and corn syrup into a deep saucepan. Stir to mix, and bring it to a boil. Cook to 310° F. on a candy thermometer, or until a small amount dropped into cold water hardens immediately and will break when you snap it.

Remove the pan from the heat and stir in the soda. Stir hard until the mixture thickens, foams, and pulls away from the pan, about 30 seconds. Don't overbeat. Pour immediately into an ungreased shallow pan. A 9 × 13-inch baking pan works well. Do not try to stir or spread it. Let it cool.

When ready to garnish the cake, remove the coffee mixture from the pan and crush it between sheets of wax paper until it has the consistency of coarse crumbs.

Split the cake into 4 layers. Beat the whipping cream with the sugar and vanilla until stiff. Spread the cream between the layers, then frost the cake with it. Cover it generously with the crushed coffee crunch, pressing it lightly into the cream with your fingers. Keep the cake refrigerated. Makes 12 to 16 servings.

# Fresh Pear Upside-Down Cake

*This homey version of an upside-down cake has a caramelized pear and brown sugar topping and a fine-textured yellow cornmeal cake underneath. It really doesn't matter which type of pear you use, as long as the fruit is fully ripe.*

Preheat the oven to 375° F.

Melt ¼ cup (½ stick) of the butter in a small saucepan, add the brown sugar, and cook, stirring constantly, until sugar is melted and mixture is thick and bubbly. Pour into an 8-inch cake pan, spreading it evenly. Peel the pears, cut them in half, and remove the core. Arrange the pear halves rounded-side-up in the caramel.

In a bowl, stir and toss together the flour, cornmeal, sugar, and baking powder. Melt the remaining 6 tablespoons of butter, and add to the flour mixture along with milk and eggs. Beat vigorously until smooth and well blended. Pour over the halves. Don't worry if some of them stick out over the batter a bit—the cake will rise to cover them. Bake for about 45 minutes, or until a toothpick inserted in the cake comes out clean. Let cool in the pan for about 5 minutes, before inverting onto a serving plate, fruit side up. Makes 6 to 8 servings.

½ cup plus 2 tablespoons (1¼ stick) butter
½ cup brown sugar
4 ripe pears
1 cup flour
½ cup cornmeal
½ cup sugar
2 teaspoons baking powder
½ cup milk
2 eggs

# Raspberry-Lemon Icebox Cake

*"Icebox" desserts are a simple and old-fashioned way of bringing back leftover or slightly stale sponge cake, pound cake, or other plain, unfrosted cake in a new and delicious guise. This one is especially summery, with red, ripe raspberries folded into a tart lemon custard, then piled into a cake-lined loaf pan. It must be made the day before, so the custard sets completely.*

1 can (14 ounces) sweetened condensed milk

3 egg yolks

⅔ cup fresh lemon juice

Grated zest of 1 lemon

1½ cups (1 half-pint basket) fresh raspberries

Pound cake, sponge cake, or angel food cake, homemade or store-bought

Combine the milk, egg yolks, lemon juice, and zest and beat until thoroughly blended. Set aside for about 15 minutes; the mixture will thicken slightly.

Meanwhile, cut the cake into strips about ¼- to ⅓-inch thick. Line an 8½×2½×4½-inch loaf pan with the strips; don't worry if the fit isn't perfect—gaps and patches won't show later on.

Fold the raspberries into the lemon mixture, then spoon into the prepared pan. If you have enough cake, lay a few more thin strips over the top, covering the custard. Cover and refrigerate overnight. The custard will thicken, but remain quite soft. Unmold the cake onto a platter or board, and cut into slices with a sharp knife. (A blunt knife will mash the cake sloppily.) Serve with whipped cream, if you wish. Makes 6 servings.

# Chocolate Chip Meringue Torte

*Don't worry if this looks terrible when it comes out of the oven. The top cracks every time, but the whipped cream spread over the top hides it and it all tastes wonderful.*

Preheat the oven to 275° F.

Toss together the crumbs, butter, and walnuts, mixing until blended. Press evenly over the bottom of a 9 × 13-inch baking pan.

Beat the egg whites and cream of tartar until they stand in droopy peaks; continue beating as you gradually add the sugar. Beat until the meringue is soft, fluffy, and slightly runny. It need not stand in peaks and should be about the consistency of commercial sour cream. Fold in the chocolate chips. Spread over the crumbs and bake for 1½ hours. The meringue will rise and crack, and the top will brown lightly. Remove from the oven and let cool to room temperature. Meanwhile, whip the cream and spread it over the torte; sprinkle with the toasted coconut. Makes 12 to 16 servings.

2 ½ cups graham cracker crumbs
½ cup (1 stick) melted butter
½ cup chopped walnuts
7 egg whites
1 teaspoon cream of tartar
1½ cups sugar
1 cup (6 ounces) semisweet chocolate chips
1 cup whipping cream
½ cup toasted coconut

---

**Q.** *Can I substitute regular milk for buttermilk in a cake recipe?*

**A.** Buttermilk is sour, and its acidity changes the chemical balance in a cake batter. When a recipe calls for buttermilk, you can make an effective substitute by adding 1 tablespoon vinegar or lemon juice to a cup of regular milk. If a cake calls for regular milk and you want to use buttermilk instead for its flavor, add ½ teaspoon baking soda to the batter for each cup of buttermilk and things should balance out nicely.

# Chewy Marbled Cupcakes

*Cupcakes are easy to eat, easy to make, and very practical to pack for a potluck, in a school lunch, or on a picnic. These marbled cakes, made with both white and dark chocolate, really don't need any frosting.*

3 eggs

1 cup sugar

4 tablespoons (½ stick) butter

3 ounces white chocolate, chopped (½ cup)

1¼ cups flour

1¼ teaspoons baking powder

¼ teaspoon salt

½ cup (3 ounces) semisweet chocolate chips

Preheat the oven to 350° F. Line cupcake pans with fluted paper baking cups.

Set a large saucepan of water on the stove and bring to a simmer. In a smaller saucepan, beat the eggs and sugar together. Add the butter and white chocolate, set the pan in the simmering water, and stir for about 2 to 3 minutes, just until butter and white chocolate melt and mixture is smooth. The mixture should be slightly warm—not hot—to your finger.

Stir together the flour, baking powder, and salt. Add to the first mixture and beat until blended. Drop in the chocolate chips and stir them in, using just a few strokes. Because the batter is slightly warm, they will begin to melt, creating a marbled look. Immediately, without blending much more, spoon the batter into the prepared pans, filling each cup about three-quarters full. Bake for about 20 minutes. These cupcakes sink slightly as they cool; it is not a flaw. Makes about 12 cupcakes.

# Chocolate Waffles

*Children will love these for breakfast. They are good with fresh fruit and even some maple syrup. Adults will probably enjoy them more for dessert, with a scoop of ice cream and some hot fudge sauce.*

**M**elt the butter and chocolate together over low heat, stirring frequently, or melt in a small bowl in a microwave oven. (When I use a microwave oven to melt, I do the chocolate alone, on about 75 percent power for about 1 minute. Then I drop in the butter and microwave about 30 seconds more.) Set aside a moment while you continue.

Combine the cake flour, sugar, baking soda, and baking powder and sift together into a large bowl. Beat the milk, egg, and vanilla together in a small cup and pour into the dry ingredients along with the chocolate mixture. Beat until blended, but don't worry if the batter isn't perfectly smooth—it will be fine when baked.

Scoop the batter into the hot waffle iron—each 4-inch waffle takes about ¼ cup of batter—and bake for about 2 minutes, or until the steaming stops and the waffle is cooked through. (Tear open the first one to be certain.) Serve hot. Leftovers can be wrapped airtight and reheated in the toaster. Makes about 10 4-inch squares.

**4 tablespoons (½ stick) butter**
**2 squares (2 ounces) unsweetened chocolate**
**2 cups cake flour or 2 cups minus 2 tablespoons white flour**
**½ cup sugar**
**1 teaspoon baking soda**
**½ teaspoon baking powder**
**1¼ cups milk**
**1 egg**
**1 teaspoon vanilla**

# Proust's Madeleines

*I baked a dozen different recipes until I came up with this melding of several favorites. It captures the rich, soft texture I like in a madeleine, perfect for munching with a cup of coffee.*

2 extra-large eggs at room
    temperature
⅔ cup sugar
1¼ cups all-purpose flour
10 tablespoons (1¼ sticks) butter
Pinch of salt
½ teaspoon vanilla extract
½ lemon, zest grated

Break the eggs into a small cup. Stir the eggs with a fork until they are smooth. Measure the sugar and flour into a mixing bowl. Stir about three-quarters of the eggs into the sugar and flour with a wooden spoon to make a thick paste. Set that aside for 10 minutes.

Meanwhile, melt the butter and let it brown lightly. Cool the melted butter until it is tepid but still liquid. Blend 4 teaspoons of the melted butter with 1 tablespoon of flour in a small bowl. Paint two madeleine pans with a very light coating of this mixture. Set the pans aside. (If you have no madeleine pans, a passable version can be made in muffin tins, but the madeleines will not have the distinctive shell-like shape.)

Add the rest of the butter to the batter, along with the remaining egg, vanilla, a few drops of lemon juice, and the grated zest of the lemon. Keep stirring the batter with a spoon until it is smooth. It will be quite thick. Let it stand for at least 1 hour to thicken further.

Preheat the oven to 375° F.

Spoon the madeleine batter like cookie dough by rounded tablespoons into the prepared pans. Bake them in the middle of the oven until they brown lightly around their edges, about 15 minutes. Pop them out onto a rack and let them cool. Store in a tightly covered container. They may also be frozen. Makes 2 dozen madeleines.

# Italian Chocolate Brownies

*Dining at the home of a friend in Tuscany, I was served these feather-light but rich chocolate wedges. The goodies have no name in Italian, but they bear a passing resemblance to American brownies, so I named them thus.*

Place the chocolate and milk in a small saucepan over low heat to melt the chocolate. Toast the hazelnuts in a pan in a 300° F. oven for 10 minutes, shaking the pan once or twice. Put the hot nuts into a clean towel, bring up the edges to enclose them, and rub them together inside the towel to remove the skins. Chop them coarsely.

Preheat the oven to 425° F.

In a large bowl, whip the egg whites until they form soft peaks. Whip in the sugar until it dissolves. Fold the chocolate and hazelnuts into the egg whites. Butter and flour a 10-inch round springform pan. Pour in the batter and bake for 30 minutes. Let the cake cool in the pan, then open the pan and cut the "brownies" into 8 to 10 wedges.

**6 ounces bittersweet or semisweet chocolate**
**2 to 3 tablespoons milk**
**6½ ounces hazelnuts (about 1 cup)**
**4 egg whites**
**6 tablespoons sugar**

# Blondies or Butterscotch Bars

*These thick, soft, and chewy bars are equally good warm from the oven or thoroughly cooled. Children love them, and they are perfect for school lunch boxes and brown bags. Even people who claim they can't bake, or don't like to bake, are successful with these. The ingredients are simple— you probably have them on your shelf now—and you won't need an electric mixer.*

10 tablespoons (1¼ sticks) butter, melted

1 box (1 pound) dark brown sugar (about 2¼ cups)

3 eggs

2¾ cups flour

2½ teaspoons baking powder

½ teaspoon salt

2 cups (12-ounce bag) semisweet chocolate chips

1 cup chopped walnuts or pecans

Preheat the oven to 325° F.

Butter a 9 × 13-inch baking pan. In a large bowl, beat the butter, sugar, and eggs until completely smooth. In another bowl, stir and toss together the flour, baking powder, and salt.

Add to the liquid mixture and beat until thoroughly combined. Stir in the chocolate chips and nuts; the batter will be quite stiff. Spread evenly in the prepared pan and bake for 25 to 30 minutes, or until the top is golden, and a toothpick inserted in the center comes out clean, or with just a few specks of moist batter on it. These bars should remain moist, so it's better to underbake a bit rather than overbake.

Place the pan on a rack to cool, and while still slightly warm cut into 1 × 3-inch bars. Store airtight, and freeze what you won't eat within two days. Makes about 36 bars.

# Crisp Oatmeal Cookies

*One day a listener called asking for a really crisp oatmeal cookie recipe. From the pile of responses that came from other helpful listeners, I synthesized this one, which has been a big favorite ever since.*

Cream the sugars and the butter until the mixture is very smooth. Blend in the egg and the vanilla. Mix in the oatmeal. Sift together the flour, baking soda, and salt. Blend that into the dough; it will be very soft. Let the dough stand for a few minutes to firm up.

Meanwhile, preheat the oven to 350° F.

Drop the dough by rounded tablespoons onto a cookie sheet, leaving 2 inches between the blobs of dough. Sprinkle each cookie with some ground nuts, pressing them into the dough and flattening the blobs at the same time. Bake the cookies for 10 minutes, until they are uniformly brown. Makes approximately 18 cookies 4½ inches in diameter.

½ cup brown sugar
½ cup white sugar
½ cup (1 stick) unsalted butter
1 egg
½ teaspoon vanilla
1½ cups oatmeal
¾ cup white flour
½ teaspoon baking soda
½ teaspoon salt
¼ to ⅓ cup ground walnuts

**Q.** *How do I get my cookies crispy instead of cakelike?*

**A.** The kind of shortening—fat—you use in the cookies has a lot to do with the texture. I once tried six versions of the same recipe of chocolate chip cookies, each one made with a different shortening. The crispest was the one made from lard. The softest was made with vegetable oil. In between, in descending order of crispness, were vegetable shortening, margarine, butter and a combination of butter and oil. The same thing happens when you change the shortening in a pie crust recipe.

Among the other things that affect the texture of the cookie is the balance of dry and moist ingredients. The drier the dough, the chewier the cookie is likely to be. The crispest cookies are those made from a dough moist enough to spread when the cookie bakes.

# Buckwheat Cardamom Shortbread

*Although this unusual shortbread won't win a prize for looks (its sandy brown dough is flecked with bits of black from the buckwheat), it more than makes up for that with its distinctive and intriguing flavor and almost creamy texture. The dough is easily mixed in a food processor.*

½ pound (2 sticks) butter
1 cup powdered sugar
1 teaspoon ground cardamom
1 cup buckwheat flour
1 cup flour

Chill the butter if you are mixing the dough in a food processor; have it at room temperature if you are mixing by hand.

In a food processor fitted with the steel blade, whirl the butter until it is smooth and creamy, scraping down the sides once or twice. Add the sugar and cardamom and process until smooth. Dump in the flours and process again until the dough is completely mixed, scraping down the sides once or twice.

If mixing by hand, beat the softened butter in a big bowl until creamy, then beat in the sugar and cardamom. Add the flours and mix until the dough is smooth—your washed hands are really the best tools for this job.

On a very lightly floured surface, shape the dough into two logs about 1½ inches in diameter and 7 to 8 inches long. Wrap in plastic wrap and chill for at least an hour—or up to several days.

Preheat the oven to 350° F.

With a thin, sharp knife, slice dough into rounds about ⅓-inch thick. Place about 1 inch apart on ungreased cookie sheets and bake for 15 minutes. Transfer to racks to cool, then store airtight. Makes about 50 cookies.

# Biscotti

*Dunk these into coffee, tea, milk, or wine. They will keep for weeks.*

Toast the almonds on a cookie sheet at 375° F. for 10 to 15 minutes. Pulverize them in a food processor, but be careful not to make nut butter.

Preheat the oven to 325° F.

Butter or oil a baking sheet. Combine the almonds, flour, sugar, baking powder, and salt in a food processor. Blend them, then mix in the butter until it is thoroughly incorporated. Blend in the eggs. The mixture will be like damp cornmeal.

Form the dough into two long loaves about 3 inches wide and no more than 1 inch thick. Place them on the baking pan. Bake for 30 minutes.

Let these small loaves cool for a few minutes, then cut them into ½-inch slices. Place the cookies on their sides on the baking sheet, leaving space between them. Bake them 15 minutes longer, or until they are golden brown. Transfer to racks to cool.

Makes about 36. Store in an airtight container.

2 cups almonds
3 cups flour
1½ cups sugar
1 teaspoon baking powder
¼ teaspoon salt
½ cup (1 stick) butter at room temperature
2 beaten eggs

# Easy Chocolate Truffles

*One of the easiest and most foolproof chocolate candies possible, one of the few that does not require knowing how to temper and dip chocolate. Although truffles should be kept refrigerated to maintain their texture, they can be packed carefully and sent to friends as gifts, except in the summer, when the heat can melt them ungracefully. Include a note saying they should be refrigerated.*

12 ounces dark sweet or semisweet
  chocolate (not milk chocolate)
4 tablespoons (½ stick) unsalted
  butter
¾ cup whipping cream
1 tablespoon plus 1 teaspoon liqueur
  (your choice)
¼ cup unsweetened cocoa

Grate or chop the chocolate into a heatproof bowl.

In a saucepan, heat the butter and cream until the butter melts. Off heat, stir in the liqueur. Grand Marnier, Cointreau, or triple sec, Frangelico (for hazelnut flavor), crème de menthe, or cherry cordial are especially good choices.

Stir the hot cream and butter into the grated chocolate. Keep whipping with a wire whisk until the mixture is very thick and holds soft peaks. Now cover the bowl and refrigerate it at least 3 hours or overnight.

To make the chocolate truffles, line a cookie sheet with wax paper. Scoop out balls with a melon baller and place them on wax paper. Freeze the balls until they are firm enough to handle without melting from the heat of your hands, about 45 minutes. Roll the chocolate balls in the cocoa and return them to the wax paper. These keep in the refrigerator for 3 weeks or in the freezer for 4 months. Makes about 24.

# Classic English Butter Toffee

*I am indebted to my friend Donna Morgan, food editor of the Salt Lake City* Tribune, *who got this recipe from a friend of hers. Donna, like me, wasn't too sure about the recipe's direction to cook the mixture until you see a "poof of smoke," but trust me. It works.*

1 cup finely chopped walnuts
8 ounces milk chocolate
2 sticks (1 cup) very fresh (or frozen) unsalted butter
¼ cup water
1 cup sugar

Butter a 10 × 15-inch cookie sheet. Sprinkle half the chopped walnuts over the surface. Break up the chocolate into small pieces and scatter half of the chocolate over the walnuts.

Now, in a heavy saucepan—not tin-lined copper—melt the butter, add the water and sugar, stir to blend the mixture well, and heat it until it boils, stirring the mixture constantly. Lower the heat to medium and continue to cook, stirring constantly, until it turns amber and—this is the part I love—a poof of smoke comes up. Be patient. This can take 10 minutes. *Note:* For the faint-hearted, the temperature on a candy thermometer should reach 300° F.

Immediately pour the mixture over the chocolate and nuts. Spread it thin with the back of a spoon or spatula. Scatter the remaining chocolate over the hot candy (it will melt), then sprinkle it with the remaining chopped nuts.

Let the candy cool completely, then break it into pieces. Stored in an airtight container in a cool place, it will keep for several months, if you can keep your hands off it that long. Makes 2 pounds.

# Secret Toffee

*The secret ingredient is a layer of unsalted soda crackers (saltines without the salt), which allows us to make this toffee without thermometers or tricky cooking processes. This toffee, with its traditional layer of brittle caramelized sugar topped with chocolate and nuts, takes only minutes to make, and everyone will think it's the real thing.*

½ cup (1 stick) butter
⅔ cup packed brown sugar
About 24 unsalted soda crackers
1½ cups (9 ounces) semisweet chocolate morsels
¾ cup finely chopped walnuts or toasted almonds

Preheat the oven to 375° F. Line the inside of a 9 × 13-inch pan with a large sheet of foil, going about 1 inch up the sides.

Melt the butter in a small saucepan, add the brown sugar, and boil rapidly until the sugar melts and becomes syrupy, about 30 seconds. Pour into the foil-lined pan. Tilt the pan to cover the bottom evenly. Arrange a layer of the soda crackers over the syrup, allowing about ⅛ inch between the crackers. Bake for 10 minutes.

Remove from the oven and immediately sprinkle the chocolate morsels and nuts over the top. Return to the oven for 1 minute more, then spread the chocolate, which will be very soft, evenly over the sugar with a rubber spatula, taking care to keep the layer of crackers intact. Refrigerate for an hour or more, until firm. Lift from the pan, peel off the foil, and break into chunks. Refrigerate for storage. Makes 1½ pounds.

# Pumpkin Candy

*Larry Forgione, chef-owner of An American Place in New York, one of the leading restaurants in the "new wave" of American cuisine, prepared these mouth-watering candies at a cooking class in Napa Valley a few years back. I have been making them every holiday season since. Use small, firm, sugar pumpkins, not the big, watery, jack-o'-lantern type. A surprisingly good substitute is butternut squash.*

P eel, seed, and remove strings from the inside of the pumpkin. Cut the pumpkin pulp into 1 × 1½-inch pieces. Place the pumpkin pieces in a saucepan, and add enough water to cover them. Bring the contents to a boil, lower the heat, and simmer the pumpkin 15 to 20 minutes. Drain and reserve the liquid.

You should have about 1½ cups of liquid. If there is too much, boil the liquid to reduce it in volume. Add the brown sugar or maple sugar to the liquid. Pour this back over the pumpkin in the saucepan and bring the mixture slowly to a boil. Lower the heat and simmer 15 minutes. Let the pumpkin pieces cool in the syrup overnight.

Next day, bring the pumpkin to a boil again and simmer for 5 minutes.

Remove the pieces from the syrup and arrange them on a wire rack over a shallow pan. The pieces should not touch. Let the pieces stand in a warm place until they are dry, or dry them in a warm oven (140° F. or less) for 3 or 4 hours.

Roll each dry piece in large granulated maple sugar or sugar in the raw. Store the candy in a cool, dry place. Do not stack or crowd them. Separate layers with wax paper. Makes 1¼ to 1½ pounds candy.

2 pounds pumpkin in the shell
1 cup brown or maple sugar
1 cup sugar in the raw or large granulated maple sugar

# Quince Candy

*Tart, ripe quinces are among the few fruits that cannot be eaten fresh out of hand. They must be cooked. A ripe quince is bright yellow and feels a bit soft when gently squeezed in the palm of your hand. When they are available fresh during autumn, I like to add a quince to a pot of apple sauce for added flavor. This classic European sweet is easily prepared on the spur of the moment.*

6 to 8 ripe quinces
Pinch salt
2 ½ cups sugar
1 envelope unflavored gelatin
Juice of 1 lemon
¼ cup cold water
¼ cup sugar

Peel, core, and coarsely chop the quinces. Put them in a heavy saucepan. Without adding water, cook them over low heat until they soften to the texture of thick apple sauce, about 15 minutes. Puree the pulp in a food processor or blender. It should measure 2 cups. Stir in the salt, 2 ½ cups of sugar, and lemon juice.

In a small bowl, sprinkle the gelatin over the cold water to soften it. After 5 minutes, stir it into the hot quince mixture.

Line a 9-inch square baking pan with wax paper. Transfer the quince mixture to the pan. It should be about ½-inch deep. Let the candy cool. It should come out like firm jelly. Turn it out onto a cutting board. Peel off the wax paper and cut the candy into 1-inch squares or diamonds. Roll each piece in the remaining sugar and store the candy in layers in a sealed container. Makes about 80 squares.

**Q.** *What is the rule for re-freezing things?*

**A.** Frozen vegetable packers probably thought they were doing their customers a favor by warning them not to re-freeze their packages, but to this day it has caused endless confusion. I can't count the times I have been asked by frightened consumers if it is safe to re-freeze vegetables, fruits, cookies, or pastries that have thawed. They are convinced the food will poison them if they freeze it again to eat later.

Relax, folks. The only foods that can harm you if they thaw unexpectedly are those made of protein—meat, fish, poultry, or eggs—and only if they warm to 40° F. or higher for more than an hour. If you know that the food never warmed to that temperature (for example, if it thawed in the refrigerator) it is safe. At least it is as safe as it would have been if it had been in the refrigerator all the time as it thawed.

Rule of thumb: If the freezer curls up and dies, but you don't know for how long, feel the food. If you feel ice crystals, you can safely re-freeze it.

Of course, every time you thaw and re-freeze food it loses some of its quality. If something thaws, try to use it up.

# APPENDIX:

# BASIC RECIPES

# Mayonnaise

*Vary the flavor of mayonnaise by using different types of oil. Corn oil or peanut oil makes a relatively bland sauce. Olive oil or walnut oil makes a more assertive one. Homemade mayonnaise keeps in the refrigerator for 1 to 2 weeks.*

1 egg or 2 egg yolks
½ teaspoon salt
Freshly ground pepper
1 heaping teaspoon Dijon mustard
Juice of ½ lemon
⅔ to 1 cup oil

In a food processor or blender, combine all the ingredients except the oil. Use just a pinch of pepper. Start the machine, and when the mixture looks smooth, start drizzling in the oil in a thin stream. After a few seconds, the mayonnaise will "catch," which means it starts to thicken. At this point, you can pour the rest of the oil a bit faster. The mayonnaise will get progressively thicker the more oil you add, so use the minimum amount of oil for a sauce that is almost pourable, more oil for a stiff sauce for spreading on sandwiches. Taste for seasoning. Makes ¾ to 1 cup.

Handmade mayonnaise has a lighter, softer texture than mayo made in a food processor or blender. Use yolks only, not a whole egg, and blend all the ingredients except the oil in a bowl with a wire whisk. Whisking constantly, start adding the oil drop by drop until the mayonnaise "catches." Then whisk in the remaining oil in a very thin stream. Use no more than ¾ cup oil for 2 egg yolks. Taste for seasoning. Makes ¾ cup.

If you put in too much oil, the sauce will separate, or "break." To remedy a broken mayonnaise, start in a clean bowl with a fresh egg yolk and a teaspoon of mustard. Start whisking in the broken mayonnaise by teaspoonful. When it "catches," spoon the broken mayo in a bit faster until it is all incorporated.

# Vinaigrette Dressing

*You will never need a packaged dressing again once you learn how to put this sauce together, which happens just about as fast as opening an envelope of mix. Vary the flavors by using different vinegars, oils, and mustards. In making a salad, only use enough dressing to coat the greens. Don't drown the lettuce.*

**2 tablespoons vinegar**
**1 heaping tablespoon Dijon mustard**
**Salt and freshly ground pepper**
**½ cup oil**

In a small bowl, whisk together the vinegar, mustard, and salt and pepper to taste. Start with about ½ teaspoon salt and a few grinds of pepper. Whisk in the oil in a thin stream. Taste for seasoning. Makes about ⅔ cup, enough to dress sufficient salad for 4 to 6.

---

**Q.** *Can I make wine vinegar from my leftover wine?*

**A.** As long as the wine has not spoiled, it can be turned into vinegar. A common misconception is that when wine spoils, it "turns to vinegar." Spoiled wine is spoiled wine. Vinegar is made from sound wine. Use dry wine; sweet wine makes strange-tasting vinegar. The trick is to start with some natural, unpasteurized vinegar (see the label's list of ingredients), which contains the acetobacter that works on the wine to turn it into vinegar. Mix it with the wine, red or white, in a glass container or crock. Do not use metal. Do not cover the container, because the acetobacter needs air to do its work. Just tie some cheesecloth over the opening to keep dust from falling in. Within a week or two, the wine will have turned to vinegar. Keep adding bits of leftover wine to keep the vinegar going.

# Chicken Broth

*I always keep several pints of this broth in the freezer, ready for use in countless recipes. It takes no longer to make a large quantity, so use the largest pot you have and load up your freezer, too. I save chicken trimmings (wing tips, necks, giblets) in freezer bags in the freezer to add to the broth. This will make enough to fill a 12-quart stockpot.*

Put the chicken parts in a stockpot of 12 quarts or more. Add water to cover by 2 or 3 inches. Bring the water to a boil. As the water comes to a boil, the protein in the chicken starts to solidify and rise to the surface in the form of a brown and white scum. Skim this off with a wire skimmer or large spoon. From time to time, stir up the chicken pieces to encourage them to release this scum.

When it comes to a boil, reduce the heat to the lowest setting.

Cut the onions into four to six pieces, leaving the skin attached. Poke a clove into two of the pieces. Cut the carrots and celery into 2-inch pieces. Add all these ingredients plus the remaining ingredients to the pot. Place the lid on the pot, leaving about a 1-inch opening. Let the stock simmer for at least 4 hours, or overnight.

Pour the stock through a sieve into an 8-quart pot or into several smaller ones. Separate the fat, using a fat separator, or chill the stock and peel off the fat, which rises to the surface. Makes 6 to 8 quarts.

Freshly made stock will be a bit hazy. To make it clearer, pour it through a sieve lined with a clean white towel.

**8 pounds chicken parts (necks, wings, backs, feet)**
**2 onions**
**2 cloves**
**2 carrots**
**2 ribs celery, including the leaves from the stalk**
**2 bay leaves**
**6 to 8 sprigs parsley**

# Basic Pie Crust

*Everyone who bakes should try making a crust by hand at least once, so you know how it's done, but once you get the knack for producing the dough in a food processor, you might never go back. Use a solid shortening for a flaky pastry; oil makes it grainy. Lard makes the flakiest pastry, followed by vegetable shortening, margarine, then butter. Because butter is tastiest, most bakers like to use a portion of butter for flavor and a portion of shortening or lard for flakiness. Experiment until you find the right balance for your taste. This makes enough for a 2-crust 8- or 9-inch pie, or a 10-inch tart shell.*

2 ¼ cups flour
Salt
1 cup solid shortening (lard, vegetable shortening, butter, margarine, or a mixture)
3 to 5 tablespoons ice water

Put the flour and a pinch of salt into a large bowl. Cut the shortening into small pieces, and add it to the pastry. Cut it in with a pastry blender or with two knives, until the mixture looks like coarse cornmeal. Blend in just enough ice water with a fork to get the dough to hold together in a rough mass. Shape the dough into a ball and let it rest for at least 10 minutes before rolling it out. Wrap the dough in wax paper and chill it first for best results.

To make the dough in a food processor, chill the shortening until it is very cold. Frozen butter works very well. Combine all the ingredients, including the 3 tablespoons of ice water, in the food processor. Pulse the machine on-and-off in one-second bursts, just until the dough comes together in a rough mass. (Do not wait until it forms a nice ball riding on top of the blades; that makes a pastry with the texture of cardboard.) Turn the dough out onto a piece of wax paper, form it into a ball, and let it rest for 10 minutes before rolling it out. Wrap and chill the dough first for best results.

Bake the crust according to recipe directions. To pre-bake a crust (this is called "baking blind"), fit it into the pan and place it in the freezer to chill for 15 minutes while you preheat the oven to 425° F. Bake 10 to 15 minutes, or until the pastry is lightly browned. Let it cool before filling. To keep the crust from puffing up while baking blind, cover it with wax paper and fill it with dry beans. Remove the beans after baking.

# Graham Cracker Crust

*Refrigerating a baked pie crust makes it soggy, so use this for pies that must be refrigerated before serving. This makes enough to line a 9-inch pie pan.*

Mix all the ingredients in a bowl with a rubber spatula, pressing it down with the spatula from time to time, until it is completely mixed. The mixture looks crumbly, but it will hold together when pressed into the pie pan.

1¼ cups graham cracker crumbs
1 tablespoon sugar
1 to 2 teaspoons ground cinnamon, ginger, or a mixture (optional)
4 tablespoons (½ stick) butter at room temperature

# INDEX